STANDING ON S{h}IFTING SAND

BY SHARON A. FOSTER

FIGHTING FOR MARRIAGE...

ONE VOW AT A TIME!

A testimony for marriages on the brink of
DE(ATH)STRUCTION and for those already dead.

-

STANDING ON S[H]IFTING SAND

Unless otherwise noted, all scriptures are from the KJV, English Standard Version, NIV. The author for emphasis had added some scripture underlining, italics or boldness, where needed.

ISBN: 9798854470827

Table of Contents

DEDICATION

I dedicate this book to my Lord and Savior Jesus Christ, for without Him this book will not be possible; as today I have put on the mind of Christ, without fear and instability, marching forward in faith knowing who He is to me and everyone who will truly put their trust in Him, no matter how maddening the circumstances and situation appears.

Philippians 4:13 (NIV): "I can do ALL this through Him, who gives me strength."

I dedicate this book to my husband; who through the pain and turmoil, helped me to become all that I was meant to be in Christ. There was tremendous purpose in my pain....

Romans 8:28(NIV): "And we know that in all things God works for the good of those who love Him, who have been called according to His purpose."

I dedicate this book to every Stander out there who is standing for their covenant. You have the right to stand for that man or woman that God has joined you with. "What He brought together; there is nothing that can tear you apart," and once we have resolved in our spirit that this is His will, then no weapon slung against your marriage in the form of another man, another woman, outside babies, narcissism, bipolar disorder, alcoholism, addictions, divorce or separation will prosper.

Matthew 19:6 (NIV): "So they are no longer two, but one flesh. Therefore, what God has joined together, let no one separate"

Isaiah 54:17 (NIV): "No weapon forged against you will prevail, and you will refute every tongue that accuses you. This is the heritage of the servants of the **LORD,** and this is their vindication from me," declares the **LORD.**

STAND FIRM in the knowledge that God has joined you together, and no weapon in the form of this present circumstances, can separate what He has brought together. Trust in His strength to keep you STANDING as His purpose for your marriage comes into fruition. As you STAND for your covenant, believe in His power to overcome all challenges before you, and our FAITHFUL GOD will bring restoration.

STAND STILL AND FIRM

FOREWORD

By Keshia Torruella

-

When **I** was approached to write this foreword, my heart brimmed with excitement, for **I** have been intimately connected with the author's journey for more than two years. **I** have had the privilege of walking alongside her throughout this path, witnessing her remarkable growth and unwavering faith in Christ, while eagerly awaiting God's promise of restoration. This has been nothing short of inspiring!

Throughout this time, **I** observed her pouring out love and selflessness to those who were hurting, using her own pain as fuel to uplift and intercede for others. She found solace in helping those in need and in the process, experienced her own miraculous healing. God's transformative power was evident in her life.

When our paths crossed, **I** was searching for a way to extend my reach and assist those whose marriages were crumbling. Overwhelmed by the task before me, **I** found support and dedication in her. She graciously stepped up to aid me in the ministry of **RESTORING AND PRESERVING MY MARRIAGE THROUGH PRAYER,** demonstrating immense loyalty and unwavering dedication. It became evident that God had specifically equipped her for this battle. She exudes power and carries a unique anointing, all the while remaining humble.

I witnessed God elevate her into a mighty warrior for **HIS KINGDOM**. Despite the challenges that often overwhelmed her, she continually sought refuge in the Father's embrace. Her trust in God and her ability to hear His voice guided her every step. Each day, GOD would give her revelations on how we should fast and pray; as she led a group of men and women, standing on the battlefield against divorce and separation. Quietly she battled her own demons, remaining resolute in her faith.

Even amid the public knowledge of her husband's actions, she found strength in the Lord, donning the full armor of God to fight for the broken. Her prayers covered her husband, pleading for mercy upon his life, while wholeheartedly trusting in God's faithfulness to fulfill His promises. Through her unwavering surrender to God's perfect ways, her marriage was restored, a testament to His faithfulness and justice [Psalm 18:30]

Seeing her battle her own flesh, during times of hurt and pain revealed the calling of God upon her life! God was with her through and through and today I am so proud to see where she has landed. God will use her testimony and this book, **STANDING ON S(H)IFTING SAND** and its forthcoming series, to minister to so many people giving them the insight and understanding on how to fight for their marriage...one prayer and fast at a time...and SEE a great turnaround in their situations! This book will instil confidence in those facing marital challenges, empowering them to trust in the will of God.

I am so thankful that I met her and that she did not give up! She will forever be my twin. I am confident that her journey and the wisdom depicted in this book will impact and transform the lives of many, offering hope, healing and restoration in their marital relationships.

Shalom,

Mrs. Keshia Torruella

ACKNOWLEDGEMENTS

I would like to acknowledge a few special people; without whom, this book will not be possible...

First and foremost, I dedicate this book to my Lord **Jesus Christ, Yeshua Hamashiach**, the conquering Lion who roared on my behalf when I had nothing left in me. Praises to Abba Father for **His Mighty Miraculous Right Hand that won this battle for me!**

I want to express my deepest gratitude **to Mrs. Keshia Torruella**, and the prayer warriors who locked arms with me when I had no breath to breathe. A heartfelt thank you to **Mrs. Jackie Morgan, Mrs. Carmen Mata, Mrs. Priya Joseph Pereira, Mrs. Sharifa Neille-Kwao** and **Mrs. Julie Allsup.** I am also eternally grateful for the powerful prayer sessions at Clubhouse with **Keshia, Eric Smith, Mrs. Kimbri Johnson, Mrs. Joanne Garceron** and **Pastor Valecia Carey.** Together, we stood in the gap not only for my marriage but theirs as well, and the entire group. No stone or weapon was left unturned in those witching hours for three months in a row! Midnight to 3:00 am! Our combative hours! A resounding **Thank you** to these mighty Supersonic Prayer Warriors!

To my children, **Stephan, Adam, Alyssa and Aidan**; as well as **Ronel, Rebecca** and **Sasha** for being my pillar when I was about to fall**... Thank you, my loves!! Mama loves all of you deeply!**

Samaria for reminding me that I needed to live when thoughts of suicide plagued my mind. **Thank you!**

I am grateful to the beautiful and anointed **Pastor Chanel Price**, who blew my mind with her great love and endless support she rendered to me while I was in Dallas, Texas... a tremendous blessing both spiritually and financially. **Thank you!**

Apostle Dr. Stanley Jack, who prophesied and fueled my desire to begin writing this book after months of procrastination. He called it out over the airwaves that God wanted me to write my book and I am forever grateful. I also want to thank his beautiful wife, **Evangelist Lady Catherine Jack** who guided me step by step through the entire process, making it much easier for me. **Thank you!**

To the collaborative efforts of **Mrs. Thercia Welcome and D'anna Roshe Smithwick** for their assistance in the designed concept of the book covers, and to **Thercia** for sponsoring the cost and for creating the Facebook page to raise awareness and to promote its launch. Your encouragement and reminders to release it in a timely manner are greatly appreciated. I know that you are patiently waiting with bated breath to devour its pages! **Thank you!**

Dr. Kendra Phillips and **Natalie Morales- Thomas** for sacrificially proofreading the manuscript and ensuring it was ready for the publishers. Your invaluable services are deeply appreciated!! **Thank you both!**

I want to especially thank and praise the exemplary services of **WPC M. SINGH (BADGE NUMBER 19030) and PC A. CELESTINE (BADGE NUMBER 21211)** for their heroic act of making a quick, lifesaving judgement call; as instead of arresting my husband, immediately took him to the hospital for emergency treatment. They were literally his guardian angels sent by God Himself to be used to save his life. Even their badge numbers hold significant meaning. WPC Singh's numbers consists of my birth date (30) and my husband's (19) while PC Celestine's numbers double the other woman's birthdate (21); and her birth month (1) ...**THANK YOU BOTH....**

And last but certainly not least, the existing ministry of **Restoring and Preserving My Marriage Through Prayer,** that continues to STAND and declare that our marriages are restored to the GLORY AND HONOR OF GOD OUR FATHER!!

To all those mentioned and those who have played a part in my journey, I offer my deepest gratitude. This book is a testament to the power of faith, prayer and the support of a community united in their belief that restoration is not only possible, but is a promise on which to stand upon. May His Name be glorified through every word and may lives be transformed by the truth shared within these pages.

PREFACE

Miracles are God's business; obedience to Him is mine.

This is easier said than to be put into actual practice, as sometimes, obedience looks like punishment. Obedience makes us believe that following it can never be God's best for us, especially when what He is saying to us makes absolutely no sense to our flesh or human reasoning. I began "standing" for my husband, when I did not know it was a "thing" or an act that someone attains to do. Who can know the human heart, when God says it is deceitful above all else and desperately wicked (Jeremiah 17:9)? What I saw coming out of my husband with these natural eyes was pure wickedness and evil; he was not the man that exchanged vows with me ten years ago (at the time of our physical separation). I wanted the pain to stop; this intense betrayal from the man that I loved more than myself was too much to bear. I asked my Father to please let me die, so that I could be released from the agony that was thrown at me out of the blue. I checked myself. Was it? Out of the blue? Did I not see in the supernatural? Did I not see into the spiritual and see all those flags that Satan was coming in to steal, to kill and destroy what God had joined together?

No, it was not out of the blue and truth be told it was not for you either. We saw it coming and chose to ignore the signs that the Holy SPIRIT was displaying on the placards of our mind. We chose to ignore them because we took for granted that our marriages cannot be touched. It is "under The Blood" so Satan cannot touch us. However, it only takes one teeny, tiny crack for the enemy to worm his way in as he roves to and fro seeking his next victim to devour. Sadly, MARRIAGES are always on his "To Do Away With" list.

Introduction

Our "suddenly" restoration day came on July 31, 2022; an almost two-year physical separation and many years enduring the tumultuous agony of living with an in-home prodigal husband! During that time, I went from it being all about **ME** and restoration, with all the pain and turmoil of being unceremoniously and unjustifiably replaced by his main counterfeit [his on and off again ex-girlfriend, ex-lover and adulteress] to finding several marriage restorations group until finally stumbling upon His humble, beautiful, and anointed daughter, Mrs. Keshia Torruella on YouTube. And that began our RESTORATION journey!

What happened in between included tumultuous ups and downs, doublemindedness, tears, fears, breakdowns, meltdowns, and shakedowns until I fled to Houston and Dallas, Texas for six months to escape the overwhelming pain and shame.

Keshia and I developed a strong friendship; twin sisters spiritually speaking, where to this day our ministry, "RESTORING AND PRESERVING MY MARRIAGE THROUGH PRAYER" is helping Standers globally.

Those years were CRAZY until we resolutely concluded that this standing process is about you and your relationship with your Father to accomplish His purpose on this earth for His Glory! We are not here just to get our spouses and our marriages back to continue to dwell in la-la land. Yes, that IS the ultimate goal but not the whole purpose of this STAND! We are called to STAND for His WILL and Way to be done on earth as it is in heaven.

Despite pleading with God multiple times for release [so that we could both move on as we could not continue (in our own strength) with the torture of Standing for someone that did the unforgivable and spoke the unlovable], clarity derived from months of praying led us to confirmation after confirmation that this is the Lord's doing. God's deep love for my husband, His one lost sheep, was evident! He knew that he was so deep in sin, pain and shame and was in immense danger, by atrocious levels of manipulation and witchcraft that I had no other choice but TO STAND. It was a calling... an admonition... a charge! From the LORD Himself!!

Standing (in faith) allows God to change you, and it is all about your relationship with HIM first. Getting yourself aligned with HIM! Your spouse and marriage are secondary in this situation.

REMINDER

Standing is for life. God's work in us, through Jesus' sacrifice and relationship with HIM, is a process to death for both you and your spouse. So be ready! RESTORATION comes suddenly and furiously! BUT... it is all worth it in the end!

Restoration is God's glory as He re-writes your story.

CHAPTER 1

RUDE AWAKENING

2012

Her eyes flew open in terror and anxiety; beads of perspiration mingling with the tears that streamed down her face. She glanced at her husband sleeping so soundly next to her with mixed feelings.... relief washed over her that it was just a dream, yet she couldn't shake the unsettling feeling of the vivid and unsettling images conjured in those recurring nightmares!!

Holy Spirit, she silently prayed, what does this mean? Her heart welled up with gratitude again, that it was only a dream... nope, a nightmare of sorts. Nevertheless, she was deeply troubled by this... *"Hey, your husband is incredibly handsome, charismatic, so very charming; has all the qualities in a 'good' catch. Why should he be faithful to you? Ha-ha..."* the enemy tauntingly highlighted!

Refusing to entertain the enemy's lies; she made a determined choice to shake off her apprehension and calm her spirit, deciding to get a cup of tea. "Satan you are a liar, get behind me.... you have no place here!" she whispered in desperate defiance. She could almost visualize the enemy smirking as he begrudgingly obeyed the authoritative Word of the Lord that she quoted.

She sat in the kitchen, the tea tasting like gritty sand, lost in thoughts, when her husband, Jonah, appeared.

"Honey love, what's the matter? I noticed your absence from the bed, babes! Are you okay?" Jonah's concerned voice broke the silence of the kitchen.

HA-HA!!! HE NEVER CALLS YOU BY NAME BECAUSE HE DOESN'T WANT TO MISTAKE YOU FOR ONE OF HIS OTHER BABES... YOU ARE SO GULLIBLE... HA HA HA!

"I'm fine, just had a nightmare, that's all. I will come back to bed in a moment," she replied, attempting to mask her unease.

Jonah studied her intently, his gaze filled with curiosity. "You keep having nightmares, practically every night. What are they about?" he inquired, genuinely wanting to understand her distress.

She hesitated briefly, then decided to open up to him, as she loathed keeping secrets, even ones as silly as this.

Taking a deep breath, she confessed, "I keep having the same dreams over and over again, and each time it becomes increasingly vivid, and I feel overwhelmed and powerless. It's about you, Jonah... and another woman."

He immediately showed offense and responded, "You are so suspicious of everything. That's why you are being tormented in your dreams... you are always giving me a woman! I have no time or energy for no one else. You give me enough trouble as it is! You think I want more problems in life? Plus, all women want is money and no woman is getting my hard-earned money. I work too hard for my money for some stupid woman to trick me into getting it. When everyone else sleeping in the night, I have to be working hard and brace the cold weather and have to sweat

18

in the day [wiping his brow for emphasis] to earn a dollar, so get those foolish thoughts out your mind because that isn't happening!"

Her eyes widened in disbelief, not believing her ears. His emphasis on money rather than obedience to God or loyalty to her left her speechless. She opened her mouth to point out his misplaced priorities, but the Holy Ghost put a check in her spirit as she remembered Proverbs 26:4, "Answer not a fool according to his folly, lest thou also be like unto him."

Truth be told, she was tired... tired of the deception that she felt in her spirit but kept being dismissed and invalidated. Weary of the arguments that erupted whenever she voiced her concerns about things that seemed off, only to have him deny her observations, making her feel like she was the crazy, paranoid one. Somehow, she knew that she was not wrong. Her intuition had been kicked into overdrive and while he said all the right things, albeit in the wrong way, his denial seemed so genuine.

"Father, I need your help," she whispered under her breath, "I can't do this on my own. I need your help... Your strength."

Jonah's tone softened slightly, his gaze tinged with a hint of pity, as he beckoned her back to bed. "What's the point?" she thought. In just two short years, the fire and spark that was so tangible between them had extinguished in their love life.

He's getting love in all the wrong places, in too many faces... taunted that foolish voice again. This time, she chose to ignore it completely. Weariness engulfed her as she allowed him to lead her back into their bedroom.

It's a game he likes to play...

Look into his angel eyes...one look and you're hypnotized...

He takes your heart and now you pay the price

LOOK into his angel eyes and you will think you are in paradise

And one day you will find out he wears a disguise

Don't look too deep into those angels' eyes

Oh no no no no

She softly plucked the chords of a familiar melody,

A song that resonated within the depths of her soul,

Its words echoed the sentiments held within her heart,

Each strum captured the emotions she could not express.

CHAPTER 2

CLOSE THAIS

VALENTINES DAY 2013

Longing for her husband's presence, she couldn't shake the reality of his prolonged absence once again. Though she understood the demands of his job, she couldn't help but feel a tinge of sadness and longing deep within her. Three years had passed swiftly, with attempts to conceive being met with consistent negative pregnancy tests.

The desire to give Jonah the gift of fatherhood consumed her, but the circumstances seemed to conspire against them. His fleeting presence made it difficult to conceive, and she knew that he too was growing weary of the struggle. They had endured the pain of a miscarriage and the harrowing experience of an ectopic pregnancy that had threatened her life. In the depths of her being, she yearned for a solution, willing to try anything.

Thoughts of him welled up in her heart. She loved Jonah so much... something about him, it was not only the looks or personality, but a 'SUNSHINE' about him that mesmerized her. She felt overwhelmed with joy that she was Mrs. Jonah Foster, even in the midst of their trials.

You're not the only fish in his pond sweetheart... that voice again!

Another red traffic lights. Frustration crept in. Geez, at this rate she would definitely be late for this very important meeting with her client.

Her heart leapt as she heard his ringtone – the song, "Next to Me" by Emeli Sande. A rush of excitement coursed through her as she answered the call.

"Hi baby, how are you? I've missed you so much. How is everything going over there in Thailand?" she enthused.

"Hey, baby! I miss you, too. Working hard as usual. The sacrifices I have to make in order to earn a dollar.... The pressure on the well was intense during my shift," he responded, launching into his familiar tirade about the challenges and dangers of his job.

Her mind began to wander, as it had heard these words countess times before. It was the same narrative, a broken record playing on repeat. She can almost predict his every line, as he described the hardships, sacrifices and perils he faced daily at his demanding profession.

As she listened to his rants, her heart filled with joy simply because he had reached out to her. It had been two long days of silence, with the excuse of a "sucky" internet connection keeping them apart. But today, he had called, and that alone made her ecstatic. The longing for his voice had become almost unbearable, especially on those days of silence.

He continued, "So I just got some internet, so I called you, babe, to find out if everything is good at home?"

Shaking herself out of her reverie just in time to hear his query. "Yes, my love. Everything is fine." She found herself disappointed that he had not acknowledged the special day and spoken the words she wanted to hear.

Feeling a pang of uncertainty, she gathered the courage to inquire, "I guess you didn't get the video I made for you to celebrate Valentine's Day?" Her voice trembled slightly, filled with anticipation.

She had painstakingly compiled a romantic video of the two of them from their courting days, their engagement, their beautiful beach wedding and first wedding anniversary - the only anniversary they had actually spent together, accompanied by the heartfelt melody of "My Valentine" by Martina McBride, it was a labor of love that she had poured her heart and soul into, as it comforted her on those long lonely nights that she can never get used to!

"Oh, shucks it's Valentine's Day? I completely forgot, baby love. Remember now, it's nighttime here so I tend to lose track of the time, babes. But Happy Valentine's Day, baby! I will make it up to you when I come home, honey love... I will put some good loving on you."

Her mind drifted, a skeptical thought slipping in, "Yeah right....so many empty promises. He knows how to say all the right things, but never follows through."

"Anyway, babes, I am so exhausted. It's been a long day.... I need to get some sleep," he said, punctuating his words with a loud yawn, perhaps with a bit of an exaggeration.

"Okay, I understand."

No, she didn't.

"You need your rest, my love. Your safety and well-being are top priority, so get some rest baby."

He responded, "Okay, baby talk to you soon. I love you."

"I love you, too." He hung up, before she completed her sentiments.

It all sounded so rushed.

That's because he has others to speak to...lol.... other people who are expecting his call...the voice mockingly sneered at her....

As she arrived at her client's location, her thoughts and emotions were in complete disarray. "Lord, I rely totally on you...please help me, Jesus." She knew that her prayer life was suffering. The realization hit her; "I don't feel as close to My Father as I used to..."

An hour later, she climbed into her vehicle. *Hmmm... let me see if my husband is online.* She opened the WhatsApp app, on her cell phone and there it was... he was online! "I thought he was super tired." She mused, a mix of curiosity and dread flooding her mind.

She checked on the people who he might be speaking to... his brother, his sister or his cousin. Nope! None of them seemed to be the recipient of his recent online activity, as their profiles indicated that they were either last seen on the app two hours ago or the day before.

What am I becoming? This man has me as a detective and snooping around to find out who he is speaking to now! I hate doing this. Why does marriage have to be so HARD? This cannot be my "Forever and Always."

Satan is sifting you like wheat.

That still, small voice intercepted her chaotic thoughts.

Told you.... You're not his only baby love.... ha-ha-ha!

That aggravatingly taunting voice screeched at her

She became enraged. She called him. He declined the call. She saw red...she composed a text, her fingers trembling as she typed, "Who are you speaking to Jonah? I thought you were going to bed?"

Her heart sank as he ignored her text.

Why do I do this to myself? Why?

Tears gushed down her cheeks, as she drove off, feeling trapped in a never-ending cycle of disappointments and confusion.... *Lord, why?*

Why can't I have a normal marriage? I love him so much, and I know that he loves me, why can't love be enough?

You worship Jonah more than you do ME.... You are consumed by this man, and this will destroy you!

She ignored that still small voice that was alerting her in what the enemy was doing to their marriage, choosing to lean on her own understanding of what was about to unfold in her life.

CHAPTER 3

T(RIPPING)

2013

She gazed out at the expanse of the breathtaking Caribbean Sea, her heart brimming with excitement. Jonah had orchestrated this romantic getaway, a brief respite of only five days before his return to Thailand. Her heart was filled with love and gratitude. As he held her hand, she felt 16 again with the thrill and exhilaration that goes with youth.

"Prepare for the landing, baby love," he said, "the plane is small so you will definitely feel the bumps."

She smiled, "I am just happy to be with you. Thank you for this. I really needed to get away from it all."

His eyes locked with hers as he gently kissed her hand, "Anything for my baby; I love you; you're mines and you mean the world to me, I love you, girlllll!"

She blushed and opened her mouth to utter the exact sentiments when the air hostess blasted over the intercom to fasten their seat belts, interrupting their intimate moment.

Don't look too deep into those angel's eyes....

Gazing out of the breathtaking view of their ocean view room at Bay Haven Resort in St Lucia, a feeling of thrill and giddiness enthralled her entire being. "This is paradise," she whispered to herself. Five days with her husband after two months apart was more than she could ask for.

"I am not going zip lining! I am terrified of heights!" she insisted to Jonah. He was the total opposite to her when it came to things of adventure. She preferred to laze around the pool reading the latest romantic novel, not hopping onto a thin thread in the sky and cascading over the island as if she had a death wish to conquer. No way!

"Okay, my love, but I have always wanted to go zip lining," he replied.

She reassured him, "You go for it baby! I will sit and wait for you."

She watched as he eagerly donned the safety gears. She literally would do anything for this man who swept her off her feet four years ago... and married her swiftly after that. He was too good to be true!

One day you will find out he wears a disguise.... oh no no no no!!

It's a mirage. He is fake.

"Can you keep my phone and wallet, baby love?"

"Of course, sweetheart," she replied.

He kissed her passionately – a promise of things to come later- turning her face beet red as luscious thoughts swirled in her head.

She looked at the time on his phone. Almost an hour gone. *Wow, this is taking longer than I thought.*

Blood drained from her face. Suddenly without her even pressing anything **'Voxer'** appeared on the phone display. Her eyes darkened as she stared at the phone screen....

That name appeared!

The name she erroneously believed was buried in his past.

The name he claimed meant nothing to him, compared to the love that he had for her.

The woman he briefly mentioned only once to her... they had a steamy love affair many years ago; she became pregnant and lost the baby, and they broke up soon after that....

She pressed the play button and almost died! The conversation that was exchanged literally made her blush and burned her ears at the same time!

She almost dropped the phone as if it were on fire, but nothing compared to the scorching she felt in her heart! She looked again. Was this an old conversation? No! This was six days ago! The day he returned from Thailand... Oh **MY GOD!** She screamed inside of her head, "He had sex with her! Not with me, **HIS WIFE**, on his return, but with **HER!**"

Oh God! Oh God!

She sobbed loudly as curious eyes slanted her way. She tried to pull herself together, but it was too much! She fell to the floor as wretched sounds of anguish poured out from her heart. This is a nightmare. We had such a wonderful three days of spice and romance. "Oh God!" is all she could muster as she wept bitterly.

A crowd of people gathered around her. "Ma'am, are you okay?"

"Yes," she muttered weakly, "...just received some bad news from home, I will be okay."

After what seemed like an eternity, Jonah sauntered into the room totally oblivious that his transgression had been discovered. Upon seeing her tear-stained face, his face dropped. He knew that she knew. How had she uncovered the code on his phone?

"Baby, what's wrong?" he feigned sheepishly. She screamed at him, "You are a stinking (expletive) liar! I hate you! You nasty, stinking cheater.... you had sex with HER! The day you came home? You lied! You claimed the flight was delayed... 'so you will be home the next day' you said instead you went to HER!"

Jonah begged her to calm down as he pulled her into a private section of the waiting area. "Please, let's talk. I love you baby. Please believe that! I never loved another woman as I have loved you! Nothing happened, okay? We were just talking nonsense! It was a thrilling sex conversation. I have never been unfaithful to you! You have to believe and trust me!!" He lied.

"WHAT! Trust a dirty liar like you! Hell no! Jonah, you cannot speak the truth! It is elusive to you! You dare not speak TRUTH. It's a stranger to you! Hah! TRUTH!!" she quickly retorted. "I don't want to hear any more of your nasty lies that's spewing from your dirty adulterous lips," she seethed. "This woman is married! She has children...you have committed double adultery!"

She continued to explode, "I am what? About the two hundredth woman on your long lines of disposable conquest, you dirty whore! One of your collateral damages in your history of permissive behavior??? If you were a woman, you would be such a slut... a close peg! Squeeze your head and open up the legs! Shame on you... I suspected you all along. Pamela tried to warn me. She said you were coming on to her... my maid of honor for crying out LOUD! And what about that woman you were messaging on our Skype account! And then you dared to change the password and ejected me, just so I won't see what you were saying or planning with her...." She sobbed even harder, echoing the depth of the agonizing pain she felt!!!

"Oh God," she cried, her voice filled with anguish "What should I do?"

Jonah continued in vain to pacify her with empty reassurances to no avail.

I will call his sister. She is a pastor... she will tell me what to do. Maybe even shed some light into this darkness she was plunged into...

All she could hear throughout the conversation with his sister were the words, "bi-polar disorder, manic depression, insatiable urge for sex..."

Wait what? My husband... my SUNSHINE...the very light of my life.... this has to be a nightmare of sorts. What or who did I marry?

"He needs to take his medication... **TEGRETOL,** without that he can trip off," his sister quipped ferociously!

Tears streamed down her face, flowing like an impassioned river. How can this unimaginable truth be her reality?

She drifted out of her chaotic thoughts, as her sister-in-law continued, "I strongly advise you to cut your trip short and return home. You will decide THEN what you wish to do. In the meanwhile, please try not to create a scene as Jonah is exceptionally obstinate, and provoking him further will only intensify his resistance! Also, what did you do to trigger him? He doesn't do these things without a cause! Did you do something? Is he questioning your loyalty and faithfulness to him? I think he believes you are still with your ex and maybe that is the reason for his behavior."

Sharon was too devastated by this new revelation to warrant that ridiculous rant by her sister-in-law, with an answer.

Don't look too deep into those angel eyes

OH NO NO NO NO....

CHAPTER 4

RIPPED IN TWO

2015

She ran to answer the phone. "Goodness," she sighed inwardly, "I can't catch a break today!" So many clients calling incessantly all day. She gasped as she saw it was the fertility clinic.

Lord, let this be good news! She silently pleaded....

After the heartbreak of experiencing two miscarriages and many failed attempts at conceiving; their last glimmer of hope resided in the IVF process. Her eggs and his sperm had been entrusted to the clinic, undergoing fertilization for the impending procedure in the next couple of days. So why were they calling now?

"Mrs. Foster?" a voice on the phone said.

"Yes," she replied anxiously.

The voice continued, "I am afraid we have some unfortunate news."

No, no, no! What happened? Jesus, help me!

"The procedure of fertilization failed. I am sorry, Mrs. Foster, but the eggs and sperm failed to merge....it was unsuccessful" .... she continued.

Why would they choose to deliver such devastating news while she was at work? She ran to the washroom and collapsed on the floor, racking sobs shaking her whole body until she felt weak and lifeless.

She hung up and called her husband.

"Make sure she takes two tablets later around 6 pm, alright? That should keep her emotions in check," the doctor instructed.

She overheard Jonah's grateful response; his voice heavy with empathy "Thanks, Doc! I really appreciate you coming over on such short notice, as you can see Sharon is a mess ... the insensitivity of them to just give her that devastating news whilst she was at work. Jesus! I feel it for her.... nothing I can say to her can comfort her now."

She felt lost, hopeless, and useless. *I wanted to give this man a child. I felt it in my spirit that this was the answer to our prayer!!! Why is it not happening? I am not getting any younger.* She loved him so much as much as the breath she breathed. *I want a little Jonah and a little Sharon, a solemnization of their forever love. God, please ease this aching pain! My five potential babies... my five precious eggs which should have been their promised twins. Gone. Forever!!*

JULY 2016

34

Gazing in the mirror, she noticed she had put on a lot of weight. Her stomach protruded, reminiscent of a woman well into her fifth month of pregnancy! The relentless growth of fibroids seemed to outpace any glimmer of hope of conception....

Ever since the devastating IVF failure the previous year, she had grown indifferent to her appearance. However, now she couldn't ignore the harsh reality of her deteriorating physical state. The nagging pain in her left leg exacerbated her misery, at times reaching unbearable levels.... not to mention the acute shortness of breath. Maybe, she thought, it's all that weight I gained. What's the point, Jonah is never at home long enough to notice anyway. It had been four years of him working on the project in Thailand, which he seemed to love, so it did not matter to her anyway. The rhythm of ten days at home and six weeks away, this was the norm now, as she had grown resigned to the lonely routine. She shrugged.

1st AUGUST 2016

As Friday approached, her anticipation soared, filled with happiness for Jonah's impending return home. However, her excitement swiftly gave way to a searing pang of pain that pierced through her body. Agony consumed her, rendering her unable to find solace or respite. Desperate for relief, she turned to painkillers, hoping they would dull the intensity of her suffering, but alas, they offered no reprieve from her distress.

7th AUGUST 2016

She awoke screaming in pain! Jonah flew up frantically. "Baby what is wrong?"

Amidst her cries she managed to muster, "My leg...my leg...the pain! Oh my God!" Jonah did not know what to do, and in his confusion, grabbed some pain ointment and began rubbing her leg only to have her scream all the more. Instantly, her entire leg ballooned and became an angry red color.

"Jesus...what is happening, Sharon?" He exclaimed, his voice trembling with fear.

"Call an ambulance!" she gasped before passing out from the pain.

As Sharon regained awareness, she found herself encompassed by a bed of vibrant flowers, her hand clasped tightly by Jonah, his expression etched with deep concern.

"Sharon, baby, how do you feel? His voice broke in genuine worry. "God, I was so terrified. I never want to feel that way again! The doctor revealed that you have deep vein thrombosis (DVT). The scans showed that your entire leg from hip to toes are infested with clots. Hundreds of blood clots!! You must remain still, as any sudden movement could dislodge them and pose a risk of stroke or pulmonary embolism. Why didn't you tell me?"

"Tell you what, Jonah? That I was in pain? I guess the ache in my heart was too much for me to notice physical pain....and, besides, what can you do? Here I am, confined to a public hospital, deemed unworthy of being taken to a private facility. Moreover, you're hardly present long enough to make a difference

We find ourselves trapped in an endless cycle of devastation, living in what feels like a hollowness, a mere façade of marriage," she concluded, her words laced with a bitter disillusionment.

CHAPTER 5

CLOSE ENCOUNTERS OF THE THAI KIND

9th JULY 2017

They both lay in bed that lazy Sunday afternoon. She scrolled through Facebook; he connected on WhatsApp as usual, sharing memes and silly jokes around.

So many friend suggestions on Facebook! Her eyes widened. *No, no, no.... what is this madness I am seeing?* A friend suggestion showcasing a photo of her husband and a very young, pretty Thai girl in a very intimate cozy embrace, sharing his last name!

"Jonah!" she screamed, shocked and bewildered. "Who is this, and why are you in this picture with her? AND why does she have your last name?"

Jonah's face drained of color as he scrambled off the bed, visibly shaken and white as a ghost.

"Honey," he pleaded, "please, try to understand. I only wanted a baby. This girl means nothing to me. I just wanted a child." He trailed off realizing that this revelation might be the last nail in the coffin in their already tumultuous marriage.

She exploded as she flew into a mad rage...lashing out at him, calling him every dirty name that was imaginable and made up a few of her own as well!

"How? When!" she exclaimed, her voice laced with anguish. Just then messenger started to ring, interrupting their chaotic exchange.... It was the Thai girl.

"Hello?" she managed to muster upon answering.

"I want to speak to my husband. Who are you? Why do you have his last name? Where is my husband? I was looking for him but saw you on Facebook bearing his name. I want to speak to my husband!" the woman said in her strong, broken Thai accent.

Sharon glanced at 'her' husband; was he even that to her? She had no words as she looked at him, he could no longer hold her gaze as his eyes dropped to the floor.

In the background, Malai, the Thai woman, cried out, "Jonah, I need to talk to you! Why you left me like this? You not answer your phone. You blocked me on WhatsApp and Line! I miss you, baby, when am I coming to see you? How can you marry me and then leave me?" She began sobbing through the phone.

Sharon slumped to the floor...disbelief, shock, anger and sadness rolled to make a tight knot in her throat as she began hyperventilating. Jonah rushed to her side with fear and trepidation. "Baby, I am so sorry," his voice dripping with remorse.

She responded to the belligerent female that was beside herself by now.

"I am his wife. Who are you?"

Malai responded, "His wife". He married me and promised to bring me to Trinidad to live with him. He left 7 months ago and I have not heard from him since."

Are you serious? Is he a bigamist now?

The weight of the realization hit her like a ton of bricks....

She continued, "He never told me he was married. He said his wife died without bearing him any children." Technically, this was correct as his former wife did die very young from an asthmatic attack.

Jonah began weeping much too ashamed to speak.

"And now look... [showing Sharon her stomach] I am pregnant with his child."

Jonah almost fainted and Sharon totally lost it. He hung up on Malai, leaving her screaming in her native language.

Sharon ran into the spare bedroom and locked the door behind her. Jonah, at the door in a minute, begged like a wounded puppy, "Baby please! I didn't mean to do this! I only wanted a baby. You can no longer give me that," he cried out, his voice saturated with regret and desperation.

Painful flashbacks

After enduring the harrowing experience of DVT and the life-threatening complications caused by her rapidly growing fibroids, it became evident that a hysterectomy was the necessary course of action. The doctors explained that an alternative procedure called myomectomy was available, but it would require private payment as it wasn't covered by insurance, prompting Jonah to decline due to the exorbitant cost involved.

As exhaustion weighed heavily upon her, the pain in her heart felt like a relentless stab of sharp daggers. The allure of death as an escape from her suffering flirted with her thoughts. She fell into a deep, troubling slumber...

She jumped out of her sleep! Her heart pounding in her chest.

Maybe, it was another one of those recurring nightmares that plagued her. She looked at her phone... literally hundreds of messages and calls from friends and family members who saw the Facebook friend suggestion on their news feed, as well, and were no doubt calling to find out what was going on.

In an act of self-preservation and a desperate bid for solace, she made a resolute decision, and deleted all her social media accounts.

CHAPTER 6

LOVE OVERBROAD

Monday 10th July 2017

Trembling with a mix of hurt and frustration, Sharon confronted Jonah, her voice quivering with emotion. "Jonah, you took away our chance," she uttered, the pain in her words echoing his insensitive comment about her perceived inability to conceive their children.

"We weren't getting pregnant... two failed IVF attempts cost me a ton of money and there was no insurance coverage. I got fed up of pumping money into a lost and hopeless situation," Jonah reasoned.

His words pierced Sharon's already shattered heart....

Lord, be my strength, was the only prayer she could utter.

Silence.

Lord, are you there?

Come to think about it. He had been pretty silent lately.

She broke out of her thoughts, "So what do you intend to do about Malai?"

Jonah's response was cold and detached. "Nothing," he replied curtly.

"Nothing? Why? She claims that she's pregnant with your child!"

Sharon couldn't fathom his nonchalance.... the sole purpose of this sexual escapade was to impregnate her, wasn't it?

With skepticism dripping with every word, Jonah responded "I am very much doubtful that it's mines. I would know. On the two occasions when you were pregnant, I fell ill."

The weight of Jonah's dismissive words only intensified her anguish and mental torture....

I NEED TO KNOW!

Months passed, marked by relentless pain and torment as Malai continued to harass them through various platforms, bombarding them with threats and unsettling, graphic images along with videos capturing intense intimate moments between Malai and Jonah, which served only to deepen her gut-wrenching anguish.

It all came crashing around her one Saturday evening as Malai sent a video depicting a tiny puppy playfully humping a giant stuffed frog. An intentional mockery of Sharon's weight.

"This is you and Jonah trying to have sex" she typed venomously. *Lord, please help me, this is too much to bear....* she sighed in total exasperation!

Silence.

Amidst this turmoil, Sharon mustered just enough courage to address her 'husband,' "Jonah, if this is your child, I want you to do right by he or she. Whatever it takes you need to be in their life. It's not fair to them that this happened and they need their father."

The words were deadly to form but she meant every word.

"I love you enough to support you in raising this child," Sharon said with a cracked note in her voice.

Jonah looked at her intently, as if seeing her for the very first time.

"You really mean that don't you? Wow, I truly do love you!" he exclaimed, as he bent to kiss her, but she moved her face so it became a peck on the cheek instead. She was not ready for that... even though it was almost nonexistent by now.

Suddenly, everything began to make sense. The moments when she caught him online, his feigned sleepiness, his "crappy" internet connection, his zeal and dedication to work - all the pieces fell smugly into place. *Yeah, he had a whole "wife" in Thailand for five years. People will never believe it!*

After all, he is 'SUNSHINE' who is adored by everyone and, to her chagrin, it's literally everyone. She shook her head in disbelief.

CHAPTER 7

FALSE ALARM

SEPTEMBER 2017

After what felt like an eternity, the baby was finally born. A beautiful blend of Trinidad and Thailand. Hah! More like a combustive disaster to her heart. The baby girl was so incredibly cute, she did not look anything like Jonah, but it could be that the mother's genes might be over powering.

Does this mean he will divorce me to marry this girl? was the obsessive thought that ravaged her torn mind. Jonah emphatically denied such intentions, but she already came to the realization that his words and promises meant nothing. In fact, his moral compass seemed to have eluded him from birth.

"I can't let go" the lyrics of the song blasted on her car radio, a perfect depiction of her inner turmoil; "torn between staying and keeping you with me... I try my hardest to break free, I'm so locked up and you've got the key... I didn't know that I could hate someone I love'...

She screamed as she raced down the highway. This marriage was driving her to the brink of madness, and it felt as though the Holy Spirit had abandoned her, leaving her in haunting silence.

The results were supposed to be in anytime now.

Sharon hired her own private investigator in Thailand, just in case, as who can be trusted? They were miles away in Trinidad, and couldn't shake off the nagging fear that Malai might hire someone to tamper with the paternity results.

Sharon trusted no one. Apparently, watching a lot of Lifetime movies marathon made her wise... or paranoid?

After days filled with restless anticipation, Sharon finally received the most incredible news! The investigative report revealed that Malai had never been pregnant. None of the regional hospitals had records matching her name. It turned out that Malai had faked the entire pregnancy, and sent baby photos of her younger sister, Rice. She probably strapped on a fake stomach too...who knows?

Jesus! It was like watching a soap opera.

Is this my life?

All I ever wanted was to be loved and cherished, while serving the Lord Jesus Christ in sincerity and in truth but here it is, she married to Casanova who was thinking with his small head; using his charisma and rugged good looks to charm every woman he encountered.

Despite the chaotic situation, Sharon's heart overflowed with gratitude as she thanked the Lord for granting her another chance to have her "forever and always."

From this point forward, *things can only get better....* she sang the popular 80's song...heaving an audible sigh of relief.

She decided then and there that they will renew their vows at their 10-year milestone, while utilizing the time until then as an opportunity to rebuild and find healing together.

God, if you are there...you're pretty silent but I know your Word says "you will never leave me nor forsake me" so I believe your word above all else.

CHAPTER 8

VACATION MODE

NOVEMBER 2019

It cannot get any better than this! Lord, I thank you!

Sharon's first trip to the U.S.A. exceeded all her expectations. She felt at "home." Yes, they had gone on vacations before in the Caribbean - St. Lucia, Barbados, Tobago - but there was something about being in international waters that felt so right. Perfect even! After two tumultuous years of trying to heal and rebuild trust, through prayer, fasting, fights and arguments, she finally believed that they were in a much better place. She ignored the tormenting memory of the high-pitched voiced threat of the young Thai woman, Malai, that he had 'married.'

"I will go to temple every May to ensure that you and Jonah will never be happy! You stole my husband and you will never have him. You can never have him." Apparently, she felt no shame or remorse at the blatant lie of her feigned pregnancy.....

Sharon stretched like a contented cat, a smile spreading across her face, eagerly anticipating the day's shopping expedition, along with whatever adventure that Jonah had planned for her. She truly loved this man with every fiber of her being. *This is what bone of my bone and flesh of my flesh truly means.* They were one, and she thanked God again for their unwavering, renewed commitment to each other. She was truly grateful and knew that nothing and no one can ever come between their union again. In fact, she was already planning their vow renewal for their 10th anniversary the following year.

She had selected the perfect songs, including her wedding march, despite cringing at a certain part of the lyrics: "Not even the gods above can separate the two of us, no nothing can come between you and I... Oh... you and I."

DECEMBER 2019

TOBAGO

Life in beautiful Tobago was simply perfect, a celebration of Jonah's birthday. Sharon had gone all out, booking a room in a breathtaking resort that exuded idyllic days and passionate nights. They reveled in each other's company and indulged in a sumptuous birthday dinner, as if their love story had been plucked straight out of the pages of the most sizzling romance novel.

Sharon had never felt such overwhelming love and adoration from this man... her husband!

The morning after his birthday, they enjoyed a lavish breakfast together and as they exited the restaurant in preparation to go to the infinity pool, the poignant sounds of the lyrics of a popular song blasted in her ears, "all good things come to an end".

Oh no devil, she warned, you aren't getting in my head. *This is the double portion restoration that we are enjoying. I had my 'JOB' moments. I paid my dues. I endured my fair share of marital trials! Leave our marriage alone...get behind me Satan!*

CHAPTER 9

A GREAT DIVIDE

MARCH 2020

What a difference three months can make! Like what happened? The world had been brought to a standstill by the relentless grip of COVID-19. What was erroneously perceived to be a rumor or a nine-day wonder, had actually plunged the entire globe into fear and chaos, even casting its dark shadow over Sharon's marriage!

After the perfect birthday celebration in Tobago, everything changed as 2020 unfolded. Jonah underwent a sudden transformation, growing distant with each passing day. His responses became increasingly aggressive, devoid of any affection. It was as if he had become a totally different person, a real-life Dr. Jekyll and Mr. Hyde. Their intimate moments had become a distant memory, fading into the abyss since his birthday three months prior.

Thoughts came in like a flood, unable to stop its waves:

Is it that woman who never seem to leave him alone?

The one she had discovered while vacationing in St. Lucia. She did not even want to formulate the name in her mind, scared that she would begin to call things that were not as if they were. He had not spoken about her since 2013. She quelled the thoughts, but the doubts still lingered.

As Sharon sat contemplating the state of her life: the chaotic disorder that had plagued their marriage for the past decade, the anniversaries passing with no acknowledgments of its significance; the growing chasm between them visibly evident with each passing day; she mustered the courage to confront

Jonah. Perhaps it was the frustration of the shutdown and the lack of income that had pushed him into this spiral. She hoped it was something as simple as that, and not the unwelcome intrusion of that woman...

Sherry Althea Gomez.

Nervously, she called out, "Jonah" ...

"Hmmmm," he responded dismissively, his gaze fixed on the television.

"Is everything okay? I am a bit worried. I don't think we are in a good place. You seem so distant, we don't communicate...we just eat, watch tv and sleep. It's like I don't know you and I am invisible to you. What is wrong? We haven't been intimate since your birthday and I am..."

She wasn't allowed to complete her concerns as he exploded in anger!

"Is that all you can think about? Sex! The world is falling apart and that's your concern? Are you some kind of sex addict? Can't you see what's happening? Bloody hell, Sharon! I haven't worked in months; our savings are dwindling and here you are obsessing about sex! I swear if the place wasn't on lockdown... I would just get out of here!" he screamed.

Sharon began sobbing. Trying to make sense of this unfounded display of anger!!

He continued his tirade, "Oh, Jesus! Here we go again with your crocodile tears. You are not fooling me with those tears. Women are too manipulative, thinking you can cry and what am I supposed to do with that? I am not falling for any tricks; women played enough tricks on me and the way I see it you are no different!"

With every spewing rant out of his mouth, came a piercing pain that gutted her to pieces. What he was accusing her of was so far from the truth. Why was she to be blamed for the many mistakes of his past relationships?

At that moment, Sharon knew that was the beginning of the end.

CHAPTER 10

HELL HATH, NO FURY

JULY 2020

It was literally hell on earth and more specifically in their home; a battleground where their fights raged with increasing intensity. Despite the restrictions imposed by the pandemic, Jonah continuously ventured out, disregarding the safety measures. He "claimed" that he was visiting a friend, or taking a drive to his hometown, a two-hour journey away. Other times, he insisted on going to his parcel of land he had bought a few years ago. Sharon used to accompany him and she thoroughly enjoyed those drives to the country side but lately, he wanted the trips to be solo, which made absolutely no sense to her, as Jonah hated driving alone.

The situation had become unbearable, a constant whirl of turbulent questions and confrontations.

 "Where have you been?" she would inquire. Her voice a mixture of concern and frustration....

"I told you where I was going!" he barked back. His tone sharp and dismissive.

Sharon knew something just wasn't right!!

"But you are leaving at the crack of dawn and not answering your phone for the entire day!" This was far from normal.

AUGUST 2020

One evening, Jonah came home later than usual reeking of alcohol. Sharon exploded and demanded that he tell her the truth.

"Is it that woman, Sherry? That woman has been nothing but trouble since day one!"

He quickly defended her, "Leave her out of this! "That woman" is not bothering you so why are you bringing her into this? You are accusing her and she is not doing anybody anything. You always giving me a woman as if I want more trouble in my life. YOU ARE ENOUGH TROUBLE!" "Besides," he continued with pure hate, "I don't owe you anything! We have no children together so I have no obligation to you."

He continued cutting her with his words, one slice after another, as she felt herself bleeding from every inflicted wound.

She could not take it anymore! In that maddening moment, Sharon hurled herself at him and he quickly defended himself from her blows. With one sweep of his leg, he knocked her left knee so that she fell crashing to the floor, knocking it out of its socket! She yelled as the excruciating pain of the disjointed knee gripped her!

She lay on the floor wailing as he taunted her, "Stop being a drama queen and get up!"

She attempted to but her knee felt like jelly. "I can't," she cried, "something is wrong. Please call the ambulance."

The pain was so unbearable as she willed herself not to pass out.

As she pleaded and begged him to believe her, that she was truly injured, his harsh words persisted as he continued to berate her with his callousness, oblivious to the gravity of the situation he had caused.

Finally, the weight of his actions seemed to dawn upon Jonah. Fear crept into his eyes, overshadowing his previous arrogance.

Realizing the severity of Sharon's injury, he frantically reached for his phone, dialing the emergency services. The minutes that followed felt like an eternity, as Sharon endured unbearable pain, clinging to consciousness and praying for relief.

The piercing sounds of the approaching ambulance shattered the silence, carrying a glimmer of hope amidst the darkness that enveloped them. They both knew that this was a tragic turning point, a stark reminder of the seemingly irreparable damage inflicted on their relationship and on Sharon's well-being. As the paramedics arrived, the reality of their shattered marriage stared them in the face, leaving them both grappling with the consequences of their actions and what it meant for them both.

SEPTEMBER 2020

She laid on the bed as streams of tears rolled down onto her pillow. The weight of their crumbling relationship pressed upon her.

This cannot continue.

Jonah had become somewhat more attentive, yet the distance between them remained palpable. She had hoped that covering up the truth about her dislocated knee would have proved something to him but Jonah was on another beat. She knew it was Sherry or another woman but he kept vehemently denying it.

As she lay bedridden for six weeks, Jonah's presence in the house increased somewhat, but he would still disappear for hours at a time.

One day he appeared in the doorway of their bedroom. "Are you ready to have lunch?" he asked.

"I am not hungry as yet," she told him. He was no chef but he knew how to whip up something here and there and she appreciated his efforts.

She queried, "Jonah, what's happening to us? What is wrong? Am I not good enough for you?" She had to address the elephant in the room.

Jonah's response shocked her, carrying with it a mixture of frustration and anger.

"You like to argue and nag me too much. I am not working and not used to being home for so long. I am frustrated that COVID-19 has shut down our offshore operations and my money is depleting. And I am honestly not happy with you."

He looked at her and continued, "but I do love you and don't want a divorce, but I think we need to take a break from each other. Separate for a while and start dating again. Rebuild trust, you know. Let's start with a clean slate."

"How can I trust you, Jonah? I only recently discovered that you took my name off from everything! And I pay all the utility bills.... It's like you are slowly erasing me from your life... wishing I didn't exist to replace me with someone else."

Jonah exploded.

Sharon, totally drained of any fight and hope, contemplated the ideas of the sabbatical from each other, recognizing the need for a reset...

ERASE AND REWIND....

The song drummed in her ears....

However, that was easier said than done, as she had nowhere to go; knowing Jonah's stinginess, she was certain that he will not be willing to pay for an apartment for her. Her job as a Marketing Executive had slowed significantly, with businesses struggling to stay afloat, and her commissions being her main source of income.

In the depths of her despair, she uttered.

Lord, please provide a way where there's no way.

CHAPTER 11

...AS A WOMAN SCORNED

NOVEMBER 6th 2020

She dropped onto her knees, wincing as residual pain ate into her kneecap as she was still healing from its dislocation three months earlier.

Father, she cried, take this marriage away as she glared at the screen in front of her. Her worst nightmare had materialized. She stared teary eyed at the itinerary- the two of them going away for his upcoming birthday. The woman he kept denying was not the source of their marital issues. The woman who is married with three grown children and two grandbabies...the woman he had been having an on again/off again affair for over 20 years. This woman that waited until he was married to get her fangs in deep.... this woman who was as ugly as sin both inside and outside yet seem to have such a stronghold over him.

Was it the illicit sex that she heard they were hungrily gushing about when she first discovered the affair in St Lucia in 2013?

Overwhelmed with anguish, she cried out, her voice filled with desperation, "Lord, free me from this marriage!"

The realization struck her like a lightning bolt.... She was tricked into leaving the comfort of her own home – the very home they shared together from the inception of their marriage. He had no intention of "rebuilding trust" or "dating"! It was a blatant lie to get her to move out without any retaliation from her.

Jonah was having an affair with Sherry all along! Memories flooded her mind of the countless times he had disappeared, moments when she had naively believed his excuses. The weight of betrayal and deceit was too much for her to bear, as she rushed to the bathroom, retching in anguish.

Her sister, Jenna had graciously offered Sharon the use of her vacant apartment; as she now lived with her son; but kept the apartment when she needed time alone. It was very small and cramped, but at least Sharon had somewhere to lay her weary head and soul. And for this she was extremely grateful.

Jonah would occasionally come over to visit her; he was supposed to come by this weekend. How could she even look at him now after all that he had done to her and their once sacred union? How could she gaze into the eyes of the man who had inflicted such profound pain, who singlehandedly seems hell bent on destroying their marriage!

YOU HAVE MADE YOUR MARRIAGE AN IDOL. I WAS NO LONGER THE CENTRE OF IT!

The voice boomed in her ears, almost deafening Sharon.

"LORD, You brought this man into my life! He has endured unimaginable traumas from his childhood, unspeakable horrors that slowly surfaced over the years. And I promised to love, honor and cherish him despite the pain! But I never intended to prioritize him above You, Father. Forgive me! This is way too much pain for me... the utter betrayal. I keep forgiving, seventy times seven, I keep turning the other cheek, and yet he rewards me with even more pain and betrayal. It feels like a never-ending cycle. There's no reprieve in sight!"

Lord, I cannot breathe, as she panicked all the more, almost turning blue in the face. Hyperventilation taking over at this point. Sharon cried, "Father, give me one second at a time. I can't even say one day at a time. One second at a time, sweet Jesus!"

She, alas, felt the soothing presence of Her Father. She did not realize that HIS tangible presence was absent up until now as she felt His warmth flooding her spirit and soul. Sharon crumbled on the floor and sobbed bitterly and there fell asleep, tossed with emotions.

"Let me die," she mumbled under her breath, "I have peace with you now, Father. Take me home. I am ready."

Her eyes flew open, her back aching from laying on the hardened floor. *So, I am not dead...* as the pain etched at her heart. "Oh, God, no! NO! I want to be dead.... why did you bring me back here? Lord, how can I face everyone? I always boasted of what an incredible man I was married to." She lamented.

People will laugh at her and gloat as she knew that they felt a bit of jealousy because she had a good life; living in a beautiful home; she had created employment for her sister, Denise, who helped her clean the house; she was able to financially take care of her mentally sick sister, Gayle, by paying for her to be in a very good facility. She drove a lovely SUV; traveled on vacations; plus, she was married to the love of her life, her soul mate, the man who her only regret was she never bore him a child... a privilege permanently taken away from her because of his stinginess.

"Father, help me! Help me! How do I get past this? Does this mean we divorce? He told me multiple times he isn't obligated to me as we have no children." He had threatened and bullied her into not fighting him for his house or anything which she would not have done anyway because when they met, she came into the marriage with nothing and she would leave with nothing. Material things never mattered to her... she just wanted to be loved.

She mused at her "life." This 'life' that was anything but abundant. Oh, she knew that God was with her at each and every step but Satan was always at the door, pouncing on her, lurking for any unguarded moment he could find.

Her mother hated her after she had become pregnant for the 16th time with Sharon. She was told that while her mom and dad were separated, her dad was drunk and raped her mom and that is how she was conceived. Her mom, 44 years old at the time, did not want any more children. She attempted to abort Sharon so many times and yet she lived through it all. Sharon's birth was breech and her mom suffered in childbirth, almost dying as the doctors tried unsuccessfully to turn her head down in the womb three times. But baby Sharon turned back every single time and was born by her feet first, almost dying, too, in the process.

Sharon's half-brother, Robbie, who was 23 years older than her, molested her from the tender age of five years old until she was ten. Her mother refused to believe her and resented her especially since that was her favorite son and the main breadwinner in the family. Her mother was a very materialistic person who loved money, to which Robbie kept her greed satisfied as he continued to buy her love.

After accepting the Lord at 16 years of age, Sharon knew she was different and felt a desire to understand her calling. She did not want to be like all the bad apples that were her siblings; those who were not a mental case, were either: a bank robber, a child molester, an adulteress, a whore monger, suffered from narcissistic disorders, a wife beater, an atheist, a Satan worshipper, or a permissive adulteress. All that summed up her unit called "FAMILY!"

Sharon became pregnant at 17 and a mom at 18, where she had to marry a man nine years older. This man was a pornographic lover of hookers who refused to work to help maintain the household. There she was with four children and no "father" for those children... just a sperm donor really, as she held down the roles of mother and father.

She lost her Daddy at the most crucial time of her life, as he helped her with her children, his only grandchildren, as they lived with him, as her "husband" never sustained his family... and her "marriage" fell apart soon after.

Now today she was battling this with her husband, the man that she knew was her husband. The one that God joined her with... this man who emotionally left the marriage years ago with his pursuit of women, before physically leaving her for this woman who has been a thorn since day one.

This is your LIFE.... doomed to failure.... you are struggling because you weren't meant to live.... Said the satanic voice.

All she ever wanted as a little girl was to be loved and understood, just as her deep capacity to love and not hate emanated in her. No matter how people hurt her, Sharon always looked for the greater good... looking to forgive and not hate because Jesus lives in her. She was told she was different – her gifting and anointing was different and required a deep CONSECRATION. God had put HIMSELF in her for His Glory!

All she ever wanted as a little girl was to be cherished, to be loved without restraint and reservation. Sharon was hooked on romance novels as she delighted in those fairy tale books.

All she ever wanted as a little girl was for someone to show her kindness and loyalty, and to never give up on her, and to be in and on their heart and mind every day. Someone there for her as she would be there for him. Was that so elusive?

All she ever wanted.... she drifted to sleep, her emotions overwhelming her.

By the end of November, she got the news that Jonah was called out to work in the U.S.A. She had never felt so relieved and happy, as she was fervently praying for their birthday rendezvous to be canceled, somehow; and here it is, he was called out to work. She smiled broadly... hah!

"May they be separated for months, Father" she prophesied. At least, he would not be physically with Sherry and Sharon would not be tormented with visions of them together.

CHAPTER 12

CAL(LED) TO STAND

FRIDAY 19TH FEBRUARY 2021

Sharon browsed the internet. *I need prayers! A word! Something!* How could she get past this pain? Why did it still feel like daggers in her heart? She felt intense agony with every drawn breath. Her soul felt battered, her spirit tormented and her heart shattered. *Jesus, help me!*

After confronting Jonah, he blocked her from his life. Not before calling her every name imaginable ... she did not even think that there were any more names that Jonah could have called her at this point! He even told her she was not his wife, was never his "true" wife, that Sherry was his "real" wife and soul mate. He even went as far to say that if anything happened to him, Sherry will be the one to take care of him as she truly loved him.

There was no longer anything left to hide. Jonah and Sherry were now a couple; in "a relationship" as she so brazenly declared to one of her sons. Sharon was left devastated as Sherry abandoned her husband, Gregory and severed all ties with her home church.

"And now, we are husband and wife!" Jonah boldly told her without flinching about declaring such lying atrocities.

She did not, could not and would not understand how this all happened. Even if he were having an affair, how crazy is it that this went from him having an affair to her being ostracized and Jonah disowning her as his wife? Justifying his actions by inferring that Adam and Eve were married by

God directly, and not a pastor. They were "married" in the spirit by God Himself!!

Thankfully, Jonah was still in the U.S.A. for work, which meant he missed spending Christmas and the January birthday with 'that woman' Sherry. It provided a temporary respite for her frantic emotions.

Continuing her frantic search for answers, Sharon stumbled upon a You Tube video featuring a beautiful young woman named Keshia Torruella who was speaking about the very issue she was just wrestling with to her Father, "How did this happen?"

Keshia spoke from the video, "Your spouse is under demonic attacks, and it is not them speaking. They are simply a mouth piece for the enemy" Suddenly, the notion shouted at her, "My husband is under witchcraft!" The realization hit her like a thousand tons of bricks. This woman "dirtied" her hands to get her husband, using dark forces to manipulate and entrap her husband. Jonah's entire life had also been plagued with demonic oppressions and entities that fought to retain a foothold upon his life!!!

She gasped at the revelation.

It made sense. Sherry was a parasite... no job, no money, no looks and no womb so she could not bear him any children, either. She understood the woman in Thailand; at least she was young and pretty and could have given Jonah a child, but what can Sherry give to him other than kinky sex? Sharon knelt and prostrated herself on the ground.

Father, this pain is too much and now this? What should I do? Lord, you have to help me! Should I divorce this man who has done nothing but bruised and crushed my heart, my soul and has me so broken that I don't even know if I can ever be whole again? I need relief, Father, please. She begged again, "Give me one second at a time. I have no strength for minutes or hours."

FIGHT FOR MY SON; AS IF YOUR LIFE DEPENDED ON IT!!!!

The voice boomed in her ear! She leapt to her feet, "What!!!? Fight... for that man that has me in this state? What about me, Lord? Don't you care about the injustice of it all? You want me to fight for an adulterous, deceitful liar, who has done this to your daughter? I thought I was special! Don't you love me? I have tried to obey you all of my life, even enduring great injustice, and now you want me to fight for this man?"

YES! FIGHT FOR MY SON!

She scrambled herself from off the floor, with new found resolution. Keshia's words resonated through the video, offering a glimmer of understanding.

Fight for my husband, but how?

Oh, she certainly wanted to fight!

Oh, yes! Give some black eyes to that woman for sure.

Oh, how she wanted to fight!

She impulsively typed in the comments on the video page, not really expecting to receive a response, but needing an outlet for her frayed emotions.

SATURDAY 20TH FEBRUARY at 9 am

Sharon checked her emails, and there it was, a response from Keshia. *Oh, this lady took the time to write to me.* And not just a line, but words upon words of encouragement, admonishing her to stand for her husband, as he was overtaken by the enemy and being sifted.

Oh wow! The words just flooded her soul as it soothed the ache she had been experiencing for months. Keshia had also sent Sharon the link to her Facebook page "RESTORING AND PRESERVING MY MARRIAGE THROUGH PRAYER."

Oh Jesus, this is the answer to my prayer! Wow! *A Facebook page dedicated to supporting and empowering me to fight this battle.*

And what a battle it became! She and Keshia soon became not just co-standers but true friends as they realized that they were like twins with similar stories, injustices, betrayals while possessing the posture and heart akin to Jesus.

To create a safe space, they initiated a WhatsApp group where they, along with about 20 other women, who were also seeking sanctity in the madness that now become their reality, met.

Prayers became their daily bread and fasting became a lifestyle as God continued to lead them, day after day, week after week to fast and pray!

Interceding for the very souls and lives of these men that were now in the bowels of the enemy's camp, as atrocity after atrocity became the norm, raining blow after blow to all the Standers. No release, relief or reprieve in sight. The more they prayed, the worst things became, not just for her but everyone in the group. Shake after shake and s(h)ifting after s(h)ifting, twenty dwindled to 11 women remaining in the group.

CHAPTER 13

MAY(HEM) MADNESS

By the end of May, Sharon was an emotional wreck! Had it not been for the constant support of the ten virtuous ladies, she surely would have been dead or in the mental institution.

April 25th marked her and Jonah's 11th anniversary. With him officially moving Sherry into their marital home! What a gift, she thought. She felt that nothing can compare to the utter betrayal of someone who was feasting whilst she was fasting.

The news came from its usual source.... Jonah's sister, the pastor. She struggled to believe that he had stooped so low.

Didn't he feel any shame? What were the neighbors thinking? Surely, they had eyes to see that she was right all along. All those screaming battles that they were privy to. Surely, they saw that she wasn't crazy as Jonah was portraying her to be.

"It's not your husband...it's the demonic entities assigned to destroy him," came the instant reminder.

She was beyond reasoning at this point. She drove to their home like a woman scorned, totally enraged by this madness. This must be a nightmare! When did this become her reality?

"FATHER!" she screamed, "wake me up from this bloody nightmare. I cannot take this anymore!"

She arrived at their home just as Jonah was unpacking his vehicle. They apparently went on a shopping spree, but Sherry was nowhere to be seen.

"Jonah, how are you?" she mustered, trying to maintain composure. The gate was locked, preventing her from entering the house... the home he bought for her... so many good and bad times.

"Why are you here Sharon?" was his instant response. Appearing scared and nervous, his face resonated fear and apprehension.

"I heard you came back to Trinidad, so came to check up on you," she offered. He looked unrecognizable – his hair long, unkempt and braided (unheard of!!) his beard scruffy and filtered with grey and his frame thin and haggard. *Is this how he is supposed to look now that he is with the love of his life?*

"Well," he retorted, "you have seen me, so you can go now. I don't want a scene, Sharon. I don't come around you, so I rather that you not bother me, okay? I have set you free to live your life. Find a new man, do whatever you please. You and I are done. I am living a new life now. You never truly made me happy and I loved you at one time but you and I are unequally yoked and as you said 'our marriage became a sham' so I am happy now. I have peace."

Each word felt like a death sentence to Sharon. She stared at him, trying to hold on to Keshia's words – that it was all demonic, not her husband. It surely looked like her husband, and the voice was definitely his. What in the world is this? Maybe all this is just an illusion. How dare he treat her as dirt! She was a diamond, a rare pearl so what did he do? He picked up a pebble in his shoe that was this witch that he chose over her. How DARE HE!

She became so enraged she only saw black all around her. Jonah looked at her intently. He knew her rage was maddening as he looked around even more anxiously. Sharon saw someone peeping through the window. "You have this nasty, stinking whore in our home! How dare you? How dare you?" she angrily bellowed at the top of her lungs.

She rattled the gate, managing to force it open, to Jonah's shock and horror! Too incensed to care, she stormed inside. He immediately blocked her from venturing into the house.

She was going to beat the DEVIL out of that Jezebel that had enchanted and charmed her husband.... HER HUSBAND! Let that cow go back to the far country to graze; back to her **own** *half dead, stupid, insipid husband Gregory!*

Jonah began wailing like a girl, "Sharon! What are you doing? You gone crazy! Someone help me, please!" He pleaded, "Someone call the police! I am being attacked! Help me, please." These were his cries to the principality and powers of the air.

He blocked her futile attempts to venture inside their home. *THEIR HOME! which this COUNTERFEIT has invaded... her space, her bed, her furniture!* She wailed, the pain too much to bear at this point, and she fell to her knees unable to stand any longer.

Moments later, two burly, buffed police officers, walked up to her and glared at her.

"Ma'am, you are trespassing. We can have you arrested!"

She was shocked.... wait what? She peered at Jonah, as he looked at her so pitifully innocent.

"Officers," he said, "this is my ex-wife. She left me last year. We are no longer together. She left on her own free will and volition, but yet she keeps harassing me and is threatening me." She could not believe her ears...the lies, the gross, outright lies! She was tricked out of her home, a diabolical plan and plot by him and the witch that was now his "wife" ... and *now she is trespassing on her own property!* She jumped out of her chaotic thoughts just in time to hear the continuous lies of the enemy.

"I am your wife. We are not divorced," she corrected him, but the officers spoke over her.

"Ma'am, you are trespassing, and he can have you arrested. So can you kindly leave with us before this gets out of hand?"

"No!" she defiantly screamed. "This is my home! He tricked me out and now he has this slut living with him who he was having an affair with all of our marriage," she tried to explain between her tears and hiccups as by now she was beyond hysterical.

The officers grabbed her by the hands and she yanked away, "This is wrong! This is bullying! Why isn't there a female officer with you? Men will always take men's sides; this is wrong!" she kept yelling.

"Ma'am," the officer responded, "you are making a fool of yourself!" By now the entire neighborhood was out in full glory.

She threw herself on the ground and began to pray aloud, "Father, this is not right! Why Lord? Why, Jonah? I swear to you today, that you and this woman will never have a moment's peace together. I put enmity between the both of you and you shall be miserable as long as you are with her! East cannot meet West, as long as you are in this adulterous relationship with her!" Sharon shrieked.

Jonah looked genuinely scared as the officers scoffed at her. "Ma'am, we need you to leave or else we will Taser you as you are uncontrollable, and you are not listening to the law. If you want to resolve this, take your husband to court and fight him for what's legally yours, but for now we are telling you to leave this property **NOW!"** Jonah began protesting in the background saying tersely "No woman isn't fighting me for this house.... let her try!"

"Jonah, you will stand there and allow them to Taser me? I am your wife...we made vows to each other. Jonah, how could you? Why did it reach to this? You know I want our marriage. You tricked me. You promised that we would date again and trust each other again. Why did you lie to me? How can you do this to us? Don't you fear God?" she pleaded.

Jonah just stared at her as if he never knew her.

"Ma'am, come with us," as the officers unceremoniously began shoving her out the gate, and bellowed at Jonah to go inside the house. He hesitated. "Go inside, sir," they reiterated, this time a bit more forcefully.

The officers locked the gate. By now Sharon was shaking and beyond reasoning. "Ma'am," one of the officers said, "it is Sharon, right?" She nodded. He continued, "Sharon, please pull yourself together! As it is you are in no condition to drive. Do you have someone you can call that can take you back? This type of behavior is unacceptable. You cannot be barging in your husband's property like this. You no longer have any rights to be here. As he said you moved out on your own free will and if you knew you wanted your marriage to work, why move out? That was a very foolish decision..." the officer ranted.

Sharon shook uncontrollably as the officers warned her if they had to come back, she would be arrested. She sat in her car and dialed her son's number for him and his girlfriend to come pick her up.

She spent the night at her son's girlfriend's apartment as they tried in vain to console her. She wanted to see no one, speak to no one. She felt dead and empty inside as the memories of the evening kept replaying in her mind.

Who is this monster that is now her husband?

Despite all the destruction he had brought upon their marriage, she always forgave him. She didn't deserve this.

Why LORD? Why!

CONTINUE TO FIGHT AND STAND FOR MY SON....

Those words were the last thing that she wanted to hear. Pain ravaged her entire body, not just her heart...

MAY 20TH

The words from her sister stung! Her sister needed her apartment back, and Sharon just had two days in which to move. My God! Can this journey get any worse? Where on earth will she go? She had no viable options! None! Her children were in no way able to house her as her eldest son lived with his in-laws. Her daughter was already crashing at a friend's house in an already tiny and cramped space. As Jonah not only kicked Sharon out the home, but her daughter, as well, for whom he had taken care of and she considered him a father figure. Her daughter was also devastated by this madness. As for her two other sons, they lived with their dad, no way was she going to stay there! Besides, his very young wife would not allow it anyway.

Father, on top of everything that is going on with me, I am now officially homeless.

CHAPTER 14

TEARWAY TO HEAVEN

The 31- day **SUPERSONIC** fast became a powerful journey guided by God. Day after day, God Supernaturally led this fast as curse after curse and stronghold after stronghold was broken off of the Standers. By now the group "Supersonic Standers" had grown from 11 to over 100 as daily people who were crying out to God for the restoration of their marriage and the redemption of their lost spouses, joined the group!

Meanwhile, she was back and forth with no fixed place of abode, having to give away most of her clothes and shoes as she was practically living out of her car. Family and friends equally became upset with her for not taking Jonah to court and being held accountable. He and Sherry were spotted all over, as pictures were sent to her of them together, and all she had left in her were tears. She had no more fight in her, as she took every battle and cry before the Lord as she lived a fasted, prayerful life. Holy and consecrated, she decided that it was God or nothing! She was in this for the long haul and whatever God said, she did. The Lord kept telling her, "This is not your fight. Let me handle this, you continue to pray for my son. DON'T PUT YOUR HANDS TO COURT!" (Isaiah 41:13)

Her former maid of honor, Pamela who claimed Jonah was coming on to her just six months after she and Jonah were married, graciously offered Sharon to stay at her apartment as she was employed as a live-in caregiver and her apartment was vacant Monday to Friday, and she just crashed at another friend Annabelle, on the weekends. Not the best of situations but at least she had a comfortable place during the week in which to fast and pray as the Lord led.

The group was in so much mourning, as daily the cries went up to heaven, lamenting and grieving as each Stander shared their stories, all horrific in their own right... many even wanting to commit suicide, as onslaught after onslaught the pain was becoming unbearable. Yet despite the pain, the group prevailed, as day by day, they unitedly believed, "the comforting touch of the Holy Spirit would hold us and heal us with the everlasting loving arms of Our Father." (Psalm 34:18)

Six of them began to meet in the app, CLUBHOUSE, as the Holy Spirit led them to pray specifically and strategically. They met from midnight to 3 a.m. crying out not just for their spouses, but the entire group's as well, also including unsaved family members AND JUST ABOUT ANYONE that the Holy Spirit would have them pray for together.

And God began to answer as in the midst of the pain and confusion, God began to heal and mend the brokenness within the group.

One of the original 10 ladies (from South Africa) had her marriage restored and the Standers rejoiced with her and helped her plan her re-marriage since her husband had divorced her. Another one, from Florida, USA, had her divorce thrown out by the judge, which was mind boggling and a miracle. Another one of the original ten, received a promotion and another got her dream job. God was doing supernatural things not just for them but inside of them, as the Standers continuously cried out to HIM and HE was faithful and true to His Word "that when we draw near to Him, He will draw near to us!" (James 4:8)

Another fast... God said 21 days. The Standers lamented, cried, and sacrificed as they put away the food FOR the meat of God's Words and Ways. It became their daily bread. They were not living by bread alone but by every Word that was proceeding out of HIS MOUTH. (Matthew 4:4)

Within that prayer season, she heard just one word!

"JULY".

My God! Does this mean that my marriage will be restored next month, were her incredulous thoughts! She felt relieved as she knew the SPIRIT of the Lord spoke those words, as she held on to that spoken promise and kept proclaiming and declaring that her marriage was on the verge of restoration, despite the impossible, improbable and insurmountable circumstances that presented itself to her.

Lies from the enemy tried to undermine her faith. She knew that Jonah was her husband, and she was prompted to put that as his name on her phone. She had impetuously put his name as "Jonah, the cheater" to which the HOLY SPIRIT admonished her many times to change. Now she moved in obedience. Jonah MY HUSBAND; it's like that up to today.

July, however, came and went by, and she grew disheartened and discouraged as signs of restoration flew past with the month. "Father, I trust you!" she thought resolutely, "Let YOU be true and every man a LIAR!" (Romans 3:4)

By August, the Standers were on revival mode, as the WhatsApp group grew exponentially. Word spread of the group and the therapy that was being experienced there. Hope and prayers were lifted to heaven. The Standers were on FIRE as God started to heal, mend, and make good on

His promises that He is near to the brokenhearted and binds up their wounds. (Psalm 147:3)

CHAPTER 15

UNHOLY GROUND

TUESDAY 31ST AUGUST 2021

Sharon was weary and her heart was heavy. SOMEHOW, she felt sick, as if she wanted to commit suicide. Her soul felt entirely dark. It was a holiday, so she had nowhere to go but drive around in her car. She also had an assignment for her job that was past due since the previous Friday, and she did not have her laptop. It was by her ex-husband's house, and she had no desire to see him, knowing he was probably gloating about her misfortune.

Her manager had already called, yelling at her about her overdue assignment and giving her until 6 pm to submit it. It was already after 3 pm, and time was running out. Reluctantly, she called her son, who informed her that his dad was not at home, so she could retrieve her laptop and complete the assignment in time.

She hurriedly completed the assignment, racing against time before his father returned. A confrontation with her ex-husband was the last thing she needed at this time. Just as Sharon began shutting down the laptop, he suddenly appeared with his very young, ditsy wife in tow, in the doorway! In her past musings, she thought this man simply had no shame, being married to a girl the exact same age as their oldest son! Not even caring that she married him for citizenship and for financial support! "Am I doing something wrong?" she sarcastically asked herself. Here it is, her husband was taking care of a lazy, uncouth Jezebel of a woman and now her ex doing the same with his wife.

Maybe I am too independent for my own good.

Immediately a sweet voice interjected – **NO! YOU ARE MINE!**

I AM JEALOUS OVER YOU.

And take care of her, He surely did. He met all her needs, in accordance to HIS riches in glory.

"What is she doing here?" he barked at their sons, Aidan and Adam. "I don't want her here; She makes Delia uncomfortable," he said, referring to his young wife, as he launched into a barrage of insults and sneering remarks.

He had no shame in the behavior he displayed and in what he was belting out. Sharon tried unsuccessfully to explain the reason she was there; however, he refused to listen as insult after insult were hurled her way while Delia looked on in sadistic pleasure.

"Besides, you are a rolling stone, just like your whorish mother; nowhere to lay your head," he scoffed, "and the man [referring to Jonah] don't even want you anymore." Her ex laughed even louder, "you see he kicked you out and have a woman living in your own home now? Ha ha! God don't sleep, girl. I am a child of the king, and God is for me. I live to see you get like a stray dog!"

Shame and agony washed over her, as the tears began flowing, as painful flashbacks of his mockery during their marriage flooded her mind. That was who he was, and he never changed, despite repeated warnings many times at various church services. He felt self-righteous in all he did, even when he committed blatant sin. She answered him with a few choice words of her own, and she knew that she was displeasing the Holy Spirit as she walked right into the trap set for her.

He laughed at her in scorn, looking at her as if she were dirt. "Get out before I call the police and have you arrested just as your precious husband had done **but** I will have them taser your @###!" he laughed.

She looked at him in pity, knowing that he was as equally deceived as Jonah. He needed the Savior, albeit his claims of being a child of the King. He was still very much entrenched in Hinduism.... his forefather's religion. He never fully embraced the fullness of God, of being a genuine son of God. Instead, became a Pharisee, portraying a form of godliness but denying GOD'S power to transform him.

Her phone rang - it was her friend Annabelle. *Lord, I don't want to talk to anyone.* She was too emotionally distraught to speak to anyone but, she mustered up the courage to answer. "Sharon," she said, "pack your bags.... we're going to Texas!" She gushed excitedly before Sharon could say anything.

"WHAT!" Sharon exclaimed in surprise. Annabelle continued, "Yes, a friend of mines from school days, Anthony is looking for assistance as he is overwhelmed with his care giving business and wants two people to come to help him. We will have our own room and all meals." She went on to explain that he couldn't pay them much due to legal restrictions.

Sharon quickly weighed the options. At least she would have somewhere stable to live for the next 6 months and, after such an awful verbal beating from her children's father, this invitation might be an answer to an unspoken prayer.

 "Let's GO!" she enthused, deciding to embark on this new adventure with hope in her heart.

CHAPTER 16

CLOSETED

SEPTEMBER 9TH 2021

They landed in Houston, grateful for a smooth and safe transition. Sharon offered up prayers for the journey and the provision of Anthony, Annabelle's friend, who had sponsored their flight. Here they were, thousands of miles away from Jonah and the painful encounter with her ex-husband.

Somehow, she felt at peace even in this scary new adventure that she had embarked upon, trusting in God's guidance and protection.

Who knows I might even meet some of my fellow "STANDERS' who were here in Texas as well. Won't that be awesome!

Her mind wandered back to the previous Saturday when she had mustered up the courage to call Jonah, surprised that it rang and he had answered, as she had previously been blocked. She had explained to Jonah that she had an opportunity to go away for six months, and out of respect for their marriage she wanted to inform him of her departure. She wanted him to be aware, without divulging too much information for him to go back to the witch and belched all of Sharon's business to her. Instinctively, she knew Sherry was a very devious, dangerous, sinister woman. Who else would be so comfortable in accepting a man throwing out his own legally married wife and be so brazen as to move into the marital home? And, furthermore, be so confident in doing it?

That woman is evil.

Upon realizing that Sherry was now living in her home, Sharon asked Jonah previously for their wedding album, sand ceremony and framed pictures. However, he revealed to her that they had burnt and destroyed everything. She was too numb to feel anything at this point.

The audacity of their actions left her feeling so sorry for Jonah, even though he caused her immense pain. It took a whole lot out of her to not lean across and hug him and to assure him that she would always be there for him, no matter what.

He told her on many occasions that he did not want to hear any words of love coming from her as he shot her down with accusations of being obsessive and narcissistic every chance he got. And frankly, she was tired of being a punching bag for everyone, as it had her emotions running on high alert.

Houston was too beautiful for words: clean streets, crisp air, and smooth roads, a stark contrast of the litter infused, potholed surfaces that passed for roadways back in her home country. It was her second visit to the United States, and she felt an inexplicable sense of belonging. Anthony explained that Houston was so vast that one could drive for three hours and still be within the city limits! She laughed, giddy with excitement, as he went on to say Texas on the whole was so independent that they were like a country apart from the rest of the country. She marveled at the thought of it, as Trinidad was so tiny; everyone seemed to know or was related to someone, hence the reason she was happy to be away for these next few months. She could be closeted away from all that drama and stress and have some form of security!

She missed her kids, but they totally understood "the why" in terms of her having to do this, especially the way in which their dad behaved with her. She swore them to secrecy to tell no one where she was... very few people knew she was away and wanted to keep it that way.

By the end of October, exhaustion had taken its toll on Sharon. The demanding work Anthony assigned them felt like slave labor. From the crack of dawn until late at night, they cared for bedridden patients, leaving her with constant back and foot pain. She reminded herself that at least she had a place to stay. However, the overwhelming workload, coupled with her longing for Jonah, made her question if she made the right decision. Communication between them had become non-existent... as if they were total strangers now. Moreover, her children had only just realized that she was not going to be home for Christmas, adding to her misery.

One Sunday afternoon in early November, she found herself alone in her tasks as Annabelle had to assist at another home due to a COVID-19 related absence of a care-giver. Sharon was on the verge of despair and felt extremely depressed. Annabelle, too, was totally fed up and was contemplating returning home.

Sharon did not have that luxury...she had nowhere to call home!

WHY LORD!! Why am I going through this?

Why do I have to clean all this poop?

I am TIRED!

As she attended to Erik; a stroke victim at only 44 years old, who was now bed bound for life... no wife, no children, but at the mercy of tired, uncaring care givers, in most instances. Her soft heart pierced to see their pain; knowing her agony paled in comparison to theirs, as these people were in palliative care, a few died under her watch, as she led them to Christ, hoping they knew and understood the significance of salvation.

She turned Erik to wipe his back, still querying WHY to the Lord, when the voice boomed in her ear...

I AM PREPARING YOU TO TAKE CARE OF YOUR HUSBAND JUST LIKE YOU ARE DOING FOR THESE PEOPLE NOW!

WHAT!

She trembled in fear.... *what do you mean Lord?*

Silence

OK....

HE MAY BE MY SON AND I LOVE HIM, BUT JONAH IS JUST LIKE HIS NAMESAKE, RUNNING FROM ME AND ONLY RUNNING TO WOMEN AND MONEY... I WILL NOT BE MOCKED.

That voice was so thunderous and authoritative! She quaked in her nurse's shoes as she quickly finished cleaning up Erik and called Annabelle and told her. She called Keshia as well who prayed with her. She called Pastor Valecia, a member of the 'STANDERS' group, who lived in Dallas and was ready at the drop of a hat to get her out of Houston and fly her over there! She had invited her to Thanksgiving and was preparing to do just that.

"You are never stuck," were her words to Sharon every time she spoke to her and told her of the injustices she was experiencing at the hands of the unscrupulous Anthony. She and Pastor Valecia prayed as well. She felt so much better for after all "in the multitude of counselors there is safety" as Proverbs 11:14 admonishes.

By mid-November, overwhelmed and exhausted, Annabelle made the difficult decision to return to Trinidad, due to stress and health issues that she began experiencing.

Sharon found herself in a predicament, not ready to go back home with the fresh wounds of her failed marriage, and she had nowhere to go. She certainly did not have enough money saved to get an apartment on her own but she could not stay as Anthony would kill her with work.

"I am bringing you over to Dallas, where you can stay with me," Pastor Valecia assured her, "we will figure something out, okay?"

"I have already booked your flight to Dallas!" she quipped.

CHAPTER 17

MOMENTOUS MOMENTS

Sharon was living her best life! Her very first Thanksgiving was superb! Pastor V, as she was fondly called, accepted her into her home as if she were a long-lost sister. She had her own room with a giant TV, and the most delicious meals she ever ate outside of her home country. That pastor could cook. By this rate she would probably gain more weight, she mused.

Thoughts of Jonah began to grow dim with each passing day, as the communication had stopped completely. She suspected that she was developing a hardened heart towards him, but at this point she really did not care. As he had said to her countless times, leave him alone, he was happy, and for her to move on without him. Maybe this was God's way of showing her to do just that.

She got a job, with the help of Pastor V's church. It paid well and she was happy for the first time in years. Thoughts of restoration looked bleak and impossible at this juncture and she decided that so be it.

C'est La Vie! She finally surrendered it all to her Father...

As Christmas approached, Sharon's excitement soared. She eagerly anticipated experiencing her first yuletide season away from her home. Although she missed her children, it was nothing compared to the prospect of Christmas in Dallas! She had already sent a barrel full of goodies to her children back home, ensuring they would have a joyful holiday season!

Christmas Eve! Wow, her absolute favorite day, with its buildup of anticipation, mingled with the excitement on everyone's faces, was priceless; she intended to fully enjoy this day. She and Pastor V had some last-minute shopping to do. She was eagerly awaiting the adventures of the day ahead...

Her phone rang. Instinctively her heart sank.

Hmmmm, who was calling this early? It was just after 6:00 am, but back home it was already 8:00 am as Texas was two hours behind. It was her sister Denise, probably calling to wish her an early Christmas blessing...LOL.

Denise was sobbing, Sharon dreaded the worst.

Gayle, their sister had just passed away in the facility... possible heart attack... years of medication had finally taken its toll on her already frail 100-pound frame. Sharon began wailing and hung up. She immediately called her sister-in-law, who prayed and comforted her. She did not want to contact Jonah, as he was just a distant memory by now; albeit the ache that still prevailed in her heart was telling a different story. She asked her sister-in-law to inform Jonah of Gayle's passing. He had been extremely supportive in the past, helping with her expenses at the home and visited her frequently. With a heavy heart, Sharon contemplated how much more pain her heart could endure. Christmas Eve would forever be etched in her memory as the day her sister went to be with Jesus, no longer bound by her mentally challenged body.

She did not hear from Jonah that day. However, early Christmas morning he sent her a short, curt message expressing his condolences. He acknowledged that Gayle was now free from suffering and for what it's worth to still try to have a merry Christmas. Sharon's response was equally as curt, with a dismissive "thank you and same to you!" She had already gotten word days before that he and Sherry had thoroughly enjoyed his birthday celebration the week before and were seen at various malls and supermarkets happily shopping in anticipation of their official first Christmas together as "husband and wife." She rolled her eyes - not willing to be yanked down that road again; her sister had just died, and she was not even present to help with the funeral arrangements. She anticipated that she may have to be the one to shoulder the financial responsibility alone, as had been the case with her parent's burials. Her siblings seemingly 'lacked' the resources to contribute, a fact that she sarcastically noted.

Pastor V was a great source of strength and comfort to her as she tried to help her overcome the pain and grief. Keshia called her frequently to check up on her, as well as the other Standers. She felt truly blessed to have such an awesome group of people who genuinely cared for her, and she them, as she considered all of them her family... solid brothers and sisters in Christ who exemplified the love of JESUS! She was truly thankful.

As the new year, 2022, began, Sharon found herself in tears, longing for home, her deceased sister, her children, and Jonah... she thought she was getting over him, but she was so wrong, as the waves of love surged back stronger than ever. The fresh gush of emotions threatened to consume her, their poignancy almost overwhelming.

Funeral arrangements were being made by her sister Denise and Sharon's daughter, Alyssa. She had already sent money to cover the funeral expenses along with a voice note to be played at Gayle's funeral. Her sons, Aidan and Stephan, planned to connect with her through video call so she could witness her sister's final sendoff. Her other son, Adam, a photographer, would record and upload the service on YouTube, creating a perpetual memorial for Gayle.

The entire process was emotionally draining but Sharon found solace in leaning on the everlasting **ARMS** of her Father, the only source of strength that carried her through those difficult times!

CHAPTER 18

WEIGHT IN THE WAIT

28th FEBRAURY 2022

It was time for Sharon to bid farewell to Pastor V, Eric (a fellow Stander), and Pastor Chanel, who had shown her so much love and kindness that she wanted to stay, as by this time she had grown to love Dallas more than her own hometown. But despite her affection for Dallas, she had to return home to Trinidad, as her children eagerly longed for her arrival. However, she couldn't help but wonder what awaited her back home... the pain, shame and humiliation that she experienced before?

OH GOD!!

Word had reached her about Jonah and Sherry's apparent happiness. She also learnt that Jonah was called out to work, this time to Thailand. She hoped he gave Sherry a dose of what she had endured during his tenure in Thailand. Sharon was actually relieved that she did not have to face them immediately upon her return. That was short-lived as thoughts of a reunited Jonah and Sherry tormented her mind.

She had not heard from him since his scant message on Christmas Day. She told herself she did not care, but knew that she was lying to herself.

She questioned why she had even returned to Trinidad, despising the place and all that it symbolized.

MARCH 2022

She felt she was propelled into the twilight zone; as since her return to Trinidad, everything became topsy turvy. She tried in vain so many times to secure an apartment before her arrival back so that she would have a place to call home. Every single time she was met with oppositions and setbacks. Now that she had the financial resources in which to have an apartment it somehow eluded her. She wondered why, as after almost two years she was still 'homeless.'

"What in the world?" she heard herself, in Keshia's tone, as that was her favorite quote.

I DON'T WANT YOU SIGNING A LONG-TERM LEASE.... YOU'RE GOING HOME SOON!

Really Lord? You actually think that I want to suffer the shame and reproach of going back there? For the neighbors to laugh! Jonah had a 'wife' living with him, the neighbors are seeing this mess.... I cannot suffer that shame, Lord! I want back my husband, but I don't want to live in that house ever again.

She had expressed similar sentiments to Keshia, Pastor V and Pastor Chanel who encouraged her that she ought not to limit God in how He would rectify the situation for her.

April 2022

By now she was becoming worn and fretful. She was literally back to square one again...no stable place in which to rest. Jonah was still in Thailand, which offered her a bit of comfort.

Their 12th wedding anniversary was coming up. She was not looking forward to that occasion, as every birthday and anniversary, caused her immeasurable pain.

In prayer that Holy Week, the Holy Spirit revealed to her that Jonah was coming back from Thailand on GOOD FRIDAY. Her heart sank, as images of a reunited Sherry and Jonah after months apart tortured her.

Father, why did I even come back to Trinidad? I hate this place and all that it entails!

She decided to attend her sister-in-law's church on that day, as the thoughts became too unbearable.

They were having a special **foot washing service** so she decided to put self aside and clothe herself with humility and wash feet. After all, Jesus knew his fate and still chose to wash feet and she was not greater than her Master.

The service was 'nice' for want of a better word as their gatherings always appeared to be devoid of the Holy Spirit's enthralling presence...**lack of love**. Hmmm, she thought, Jonah's sister did operate in a lot of unforgiveness and hate.

They gave out tokens of small bottles of 'anointing' oil. Sharon ended up with two for some reason, so she kept one in her car, and kept one at her "home" where she was currently crashing.

As Saturday approached, anxiety filled her heart. Did Jonah really come back? *Well, call his number and find out,* was the thought that popped into her head. If the phone rang, he was back, and if it went straight to voicemail, then he was not.

She hesitated, but the feeling of having to know took precedence over everything else so with a pounding heart she dialed 'Jonah MY HUSBAND' on her phone.

It RANG!

So, he was back, just as the Holy Spirit had revealed to her days before!

About to hang up, she was floored by Jonah's gruff voice on the other end of the line. Oh no! She was not ready for this encounter.

"Yes, Sharon. What do you want this time?" Was his rude inquiry.

This time? She hadn't spoken to him in like forever.

She laughed sheepishly. "It seems that I am on your welcome home committee, always here to herald your arrival," she offered, blushing as she remembered the last 'welcome home' episode.

Apparently, he remembered, too, as he barked, "Don't you dare think to come here to embarrass me again!!

She interrupted him rudely, "Or what? You will have me arrested this time?"

He exploded, "Sharon, why are you calling? Really, why are you? Did I not tell you to move on, your escapades in Texas weren't enough? I AM SURE that you had fun with all types of men. They weren't enough for your foolish games you keep playing? Leave me alone... Drink water and go mind your business! You are still so obsessive over me, it's not love! You have me scared because you are narcissistic and crazy. Don't come around me or Sherry, okay?" he warned.

Father, why do I keep doing this to myself. This man obviously hates me for God knows what?

What Lord? she asked facetiously.

He growled the more, as he continued, "How did you know I was home? My sister told you?"

"Your sister knew?" Sharon queried, as his sister had asked her after service, yesterday, when was her brother coming home.... so, she doubted that she had a clue.

"No. I told no one except Sherry," Jonah said quickly

She responded, "Well, then how could she have told me?"

"The Holy Spirit told me." She admitted.

Jonah continued with his cutting words, "Hah! Why are you always lying? God sees and knows all things!"

She quickly interrupted him, "Yes, Jonah... well said."

"God sees and knows EVERYTHING!" she emphatically whispered, to which Jonah had no response.

"Jonah," she continued, "the Lord also showed me that you and Sherry will be in a very bad accident and she will die and you will live but be paralyzed. He says He has been speaking to you about your sinful lifestyle, but you refuse to listen."

He cut her off, "I rebuke that in the name of Jesus! I refuse that curse you are putting on us. God is a good God! God is on the positive side and has always been good to me, and He is not going to allow it!!"

Jonah shouted, trying to convince himself.

"Anyway, Sharon if you have nothing else to do but call and harass me and to put curses on me like the witch that you are, busy serving your father Satan, I have better things to do as I am very busy. Goodbye!"

He hung up on her without waiting for her response.

Sharon spent the days leading up to her anniversary in prayer and fasting with Keshia. On the date of their anniversary, the LORD spoke these comforting scriptures over her "Those who stand firm during testing are blessed.

They are tried and true. They will receive the life God has promised to those who love Him as their reward'. [James 1:12]

The LORD also told her that she ought not to fixate on Sherry, but rather feel sorry for her; as she came into Jonah's life to divert him away from God's purpose; used as an instrument of Satan, collaborating with demonic entities to lead Jonah down a dark, perilous road of sexual lust and perversion because Sherry will do **ANYTHING FOR MONEY**. He then explicitly revealed to her one of the tactics that Sherry used in which to lure Jonah for all these years...a disgusting thing that she did with her three-day used underwear in making a hot beverage for him. As well as in the food she had cooked for him. God will not overlook that for much longer. HE said her days were numbered...Sherry was also being used so that Jonah can see Sharon's value in his life; all were the reassuring thoughts downloaded to her spirit.

Start praying for mercy to triumph over judgment..James 2:13... she heard so emphatically. **Pray for mercy as my judgement is about to fall. I REFUSE TO BE MOCKED!**

She had to warn Jonah, of the calamity about to befall him. She pleaded, "God, don't let him die. You promised restoration. I know that Jonah is taking your longsuffering with him for granted, but please, Lord, gave us a second chance at love and I promise that we will both fulfill the calling that you have placed upon us!" She continued her vow, "We will fulfill the call and show the nations what a great and magnificent God that you are!"

The next two months, met Sharon and Keshia in continuous prayer and fasting as together they began to intercede as the Lord would lead. It was a mixture of excitement and apprehension, as they both knew that something was about to explode in the Spiritual realms.

CHAPTER 19

AND THEN......SUDDENLY

JUNE 2022

After completing another season of prayer and fasting, Sharon received an unexpected invitation to travel to London, England!

She loved England.

She was actually supposed to be living there had her mother taken up a visiting head nurse's offer to adopt her. She always regretted that her mom opted to keep her instead.

I guess she wanted me to suffer and not have a good life. Her mom had contracted tuberculosis after her birth and had to be hospitalized for six months. The nurse saw her picture at her mom's bedside and wanted her, but her mom refused.

Excited about the journey, Sharon couldn't help but envision herself speaking with a British accent, jokingly declaring that she would never stop talking if she ever acquired one. However, amidst her anticipation, Jonah's actions continued to distance and alienate her. Rumors of his official commitment to Sherry, introducing her to family and friends as his 'wife'; parading her so proudly, pierced her heart. She felt weary from the ongoing struggle, as restoration, a promise she had fervently prayed for and professed, seemed elusive and contradictory in the face of such circumstances.

DO YOU TRUST ME?

GOD, I do, but....

IT'S EITHER YOU TRUST WHAT I AM DOING OR YOU DO NOT?

This was the firm response she received from God.

She pursed her lip. *Well, either way I am going to England, so Jonah can keep on living his sinful life... I am done!*

By now she was completely ignoring the calls of her sister-in-law as after speaking to her, many a time, Sharon became more distraught from the constant barrage of bad news. From the very wise advice from Keshia, it was time to shut her out! Her sister-in- law confused Sharon as she said that she was agreeing with her in praying for restoration between Sharon and her brother, but yet told her things to drive a deeper wedge between Jonah and herself. At one point, she even told the vicious lie that Sherry made a better wife to Jonah as Sherry was submissive and Sharon way too boisterous. Well, Sherry was incidentally her sister-in-law's longtime friend and maybe she still looked at her favorably. She even began dropping hints to Sharon to divorce her brother... to take what she can get from him. Because as she declared... "you have some serious ammunitions against him" and move on with her life.

Sharon's birthday arrived, and to her disappointment, Jonah did not even send a greeting or text. She could not believe that he was so hostile towards her that she did not even warrant a "Happy Birthday!" What did she expect? As she had told the LORD days before, she was done. *I will still pray for him, but I am not going to pray for "us" anymore.*

She was anticipating the sponsors booking her flight and she hightailing it out of Trinidad again for another six months. Jonah can have the witch. Let his "wife" and he live their life in pieces because the Word of God says there is no peace unto the wicked!

JULY 2022

She received the devastating news that the deal with the sponsors fell through, therefore squashing her plans and dreams of heading to England for the next six months. She fell into a deep depression that had her questioning God yet again.

I think you like to see me like this. Pining for a man that doesn't want me.

Jonah, she thought, wishes that she disappeared off the planet, so he could live peacefully with his "princess".

Despite their fractured relationship, Jonah hadn't pursued a divorce for two reasons. Firstly, he was benefitting financially from being married to Sharon, receiving a monthly stipend of $300.00 US under the new contract from his employers issued just before the COVID-19 shutdown/their separation, and he wasn't about to give that up. Jonah's love for money outweighed his concern for people! Secondly, Jonah knew that Sharon possessed damaging information about his numerous sexual escapades, which could result in significant financial losses for him due to the country's stringent laws. However, unknown to Jonah, she was already mandated by the Lord to NOT pursue any legal battles with Jonah.

HE will fix and vindicate.

In the midst of her struggles, the LORD spoke to her, instructing her to buy sand for her vow renewal ceremony!

Okay, Lord! If you say so.

Do I get the vase too? You know that Jonah destroyed everything from our marriage ceremony. Vase, sand, everything was tossed, just as he tossed me aside!!!

She was actually being sarcastic, as she felt that weariness was overtaking her at this point.

NO! JUST THE SAND

The same colors as before? (Referring to her previous colors that Jonah threw away).

(Oh, HE was really speaking to her....)

NO! Your color, Jonah's color and my royal color!

Which is?

Your birth stone color, (PEARL) Jonah's birthstone color (TURQUIOSE) and my royal color HE repeated

Your royal color, Lord?

PURPLE

Okay, she thought, submissively.

Meanwhile, Sharon and Keshia continued their ministry, as they relentlessly contended for the group which consisted of over a thousand followers on Facebook and a daily growing WhatsApp group that had to be separated into several channels: New Stander, Seasoned Stander, Prayer Warriors, Proverbs 31 wives, Men of Fire and ADMINS. Somedays were exhaustive; but very rewarding as they continued to pray, pour and praise over God's people. Sharon's prayers had become laser-focused on Jonah's salvation and protection, leaving everything else in God's Mighty Hands.

Her sister-in-law's birthday was fast approaching. Sharon decided to drop off her gifts a week in advance, hating to go into the area, as Jonah lived not too far away and wanted to avoid him like the plague at this point.

Thursday 21st July 2022

Of course, her sister-in-law couldn't resist bringing up Jonah and lamenting about his sinful lifestyle with "this woman". Sharon couldn't escape the conversation, and to add to her annoyance, she heard that Sherry was now taking care of her grandbabies, with Jonah's assistance. The bitterness from the failed trip to England still lingered within Sharon, intensifying her disinterest in these updates. In a brusque tone, she made it clear that she didn't care about the situation, her frustration palpable. With a hasty excuse about being late for a meeting, she swiftly bade her sister-in-law farewell and drove off, seeking solace from the mounting emotions that weighed upon her.

Saturday 23rd July 2022

Her children decided to treat her to a local concert, insisting that she needed some youthful energy and excitement in her life. They playfully teased her, calling her 'boring' due to her dedication to prayer and fasting. Although it was technically a belated celebration since they hadn't done anything significant for her birthday, she reluctantly agreed to join them.

She surprisingly had fun, and by the time she got home at 2:00 am, she was totally exhausted. In moments like these, she was reminded of the importance of embracing moments of joy and rejuvenation. Ecclesiastes 3:4 reminds us, "There is a time to weep and a time to laugh, a time to mourn and a time to dance".

She smiled before drifting to sleep. Grateful for the unexpected joy that her children had brought into her life.

Sunday 24th July, 2022

6:30 AM

She awoke, groggy but with a restlessness in her spirit. Something was amiss!

She checked her phone.

15 what's app messages from Jonah!

He never ever texted her, unless it was for something significant pertaining to work or a legal matter that was ongoing for the house, unrelated to their marriage. Curiosity and anticipation filled her as she hastily opened the messages, reading the subliminal words that conveyed a profound realization on his part. Jonah was apologizing for everything that had transpired between them. Overwhelmed with emotion, Sharon couldn't help but burst into tears. She immediately called Keshia, whose own tears mirrored her own!

However, among his messages, Jonah had mentioned not to contact or call him unless he reached out again. What did that even mean? He asked her to keep him in prayer as he was experiencing a transformative encounter and needed their intercession.

Hmmm what was happening?

Was restoration happening....

What is happening?

In response to Jonah's plea for prayer, she and Keshia resolved to embark on a 3-day fast, following in the footsteps of Queen Esther who sought God's intervention for her people. With unwavering determination, they prepared to engage in another spiritual battle, knowing that they were assigned to defy the schemes of the enemy. They were ready to stand firm and release the power of prayer to overcome any opposition that might arise.

As they entered into this season of intensified prayer and fasting, they held onto the words of 2 Corinthians 10:4, which reminds us that "the weapons of our warfare are not of the flesh but have divine power to destroy strongholds." They were prepared to unleash the power of prayer to see God's miraculous Hand at work!!!

They prepared to set 10,000 to flight!"

What was about to unfold was JUST UNBELIEVABLE!!

CHAPTER 20

WHAT IS HAPPENING

Monday 25th July 2022 at 9:30 am

In the midst of her virtual work meeting, her phone rings; Sharon glanced at it and her heart somersaulted as she saw "Jonah, MY HUSBAND" displayed on the screen.

Oh, my goodness, what should I say?

She was not ready for this! After years of antagonism and enduring abuse, how could she handle a changed Jonah, who may be gentle and contrite? Not even sure if that was the case or what was happening, she answered him with a soft, gentle "Hi."

"Hello stranger!" Jonah enthused; his tone filled with an unusual happiness. "How are you?"

Sharon replied with her customary response, "Blessed and highly favored," a phrase she often used when asked about her well-being...

Their conversation meandered for about ten minutes, skirting around the core issues of his sins, their separation, and the turmoil that had consumed their lives for the past few years. Sharon chose not to press the matter or make it a big deal, opting instead for polite exchanges.

"Will you be attending my sister's thanksgiving ceremony for her birthday?"

"I wasn't invited," she revealed. Shocked; as his sister had told her she wasn't doing anything significant for her birthday!

"Well, I want you there."

Wait.... what? What about Sherry?

She dared not ask him.

"Well, I think that is up to your sister, as I am sure she didn't invite me because she wants you there, as well as Roland." (Their brother who was pleased that she and Jonah had split up and was highly endorsing his relationship with Sherry).

"Call her and tell her that I want you there," Jonah insisted.

"Uhm, ok. I will call her." Sharon agreed, totally numb by this unfolding scenario....

"And, Sharon, dress up and look pretty!" The shock of this request almost caused her to faint!

She responded, "Oh, okay. Sure."

"Great! See you on Sunday," Jonah concluded before ending the call.

She forgot all about the work meeting entirely, as she immediately called Keshia, who began crying again.

What in the world?

She also called, Pastor V and Pastor Chanel who began praising God and said they would continue in prayer for God to do what only He can do! Sharon clung to their prayers and support, sensing that it was GOD alone who could orchestrate such a sudden, surprising turn of events. Was this the beginning of the supernatural miracle of restoration?

Yet, during her excitement, a feeling of unease gripped her. There was an underlying sense that something else was transpiring, and the LORD had chosen to remain silent.

She called her sister-in-law, to share the news....

"WHAT? He called you?" was her shocked response. She became upset that Jonah had revealed her plans for a big celebration after deliberately lying to Sharon about it.

His sister flipped, "has he gone mad or something...only last Friday we spoke!"

Oh really, I thought you do not communicate.

"And he demanded that you not be there or else he and Roland will not attend, and then he had Roland call me to say the same thing! Don't be playing matchmaker and invite "her" because I will walk out the service; was his warning to me....and that is the only reason I didn't tell you Sharon."

She was nonplussed as only three days ago; he expressed hate about her to his sister. On Sunday morning, Jonah messaged her with these messages that did not make much sense and today called her to invite her to his sister's thanksgiving which he emphatically told his sister to make sure she doesn't attend? WOW!

"Can't you see he is thinking from a depraved mind, Sharon? Jonah is going crazy and he need to take his medication," she continued seeming quite perturbed by this sudden change of events.

"I am not going to attend," Sharon replied, "I am not sure what's going on, and I don't want to be embarrassed." By now she could not trust Jonah. Suppose he wanted to parade Sherry around and humiliate her even further now? Furthermore, she was not included on the invitation list.

His sister told her that she was welcome as she wanted her there in the first place, so she was actually happy that Jonah wanted her to attend.

However, Keshia admonished Sharon not to let pride guide her decision. Keshia advised her that attending was a spiritual victory against the spirit of pride. Sharon remained stubborn but promised to contemplate it further.

Keshia warned her, playfully but with a serious undertone "Girl, you better not let me hop on a plane and come shake some sense into you! Your husband is being worked on by the Holy Spirit; he is turning back to God and to you, so keep praying and believing God for full restoration."

Sharon promised to keep God at the center of it all and whatever He said she would surely do.

SILENCE.... from her Father and Jonah all of that week. This is just too crazy.

"WHAT IS HAPPENING?" were her frantic thoughts the entire week.

Did she imagine the phone call from Jonah? He asked her to not call or message unless he contacted her first. Were Sherry and he done? Was she still living with him? The excessive thoughts flooded her mind so that she could barely function.

Later that day, her son called her visibly upset. Her sister, Denise, had called his wife, her daughter-in-law, and told them that Sharon was working spells and witchcraft to gain her husband back. *What?!!* She recalled the words of her Heavenly Father two weeks before, that he was about to unmask all the snakes and scorpions in her life. Her sister who she had been so good to? Created employment for her as no one wanted to hire her due to her bad knees. She already had turned her entire siblings against her, over the years, very subtly and subliminally. She did betray her years ago when she told Jonah a lot of lies about her, but she had repented and told her she had changed. Now Stephan was angrily saying that his mother-in-law had believed her and now Sharon was no longer welcomed in her home. "LET HER KEEP AWAY FROM ME!" was her very angry, unfounded message to her. Sharon saw the enemy's plan to create division in the family. *Not today Satan.... you better move!*

She called her sister, who started gaslighting her, telling her that **she was** working witchcraft, and she felt she was "too good, you feel you are a "goody two shoes" and everyone should be afraid of you because "you always praying" she stated sarcastically with evil dripping out of every syllable. "Precious Sharon.... never thought your husband will leave you for a frumpy old fowl, right?" she laughed hysterically.

Sharon could not believe the sudden change in her sister. It was so demonic and blatantly so. *Satan you really moving around seeking who you can devour! Just wow!*

Get beneath me! You have no power! Fire of the Holy Ghost, come now and incinerate your dirty devious plans and schemes...you bite the dust now!! Angel of God, swipe up the enemy's agenda and move it away as far as the east is from the west! No power Satan.... get out!

She began to battle in prayer, weeping in the process as the utter betrayal of what her sister did **AGAIN** became her harsh reality! The thing is, she truly loved this sister as a mother, as she took care of Sharon growing up, being 13 years older that Sharon. She was always considered the baby of the family and they treated her as such up to today.

WHAT IS HAPPENING?

CHAPTER 21

WHAT HAPPENED?

SATURDAY 30ᵀᴴ JULY 2022

Sharon decided to pamper herself with a manicure and pedicure. Though she had no particular reason for doing so, she couldn't escape the weight of uncertainty looming over her. The Thanksgiving celebration for her sister-in-law was scheduled for the next morning, but she was still undecided about attending. Even Keshia's encouragement to surrender to God's will did little to appease her mounting apprehension. Jonah was silent, absolutely no communication from him since that sole phone call on Monday. Even the Holy Spirit seemed distant and unresponsive.

In her confusion, she chose to observe a day of fasting, willingly waiting to hear from both God and her husband.... surely, Jonah will at least call her to confirm her attendance tomorrow....

She went to bed around 10:00 pm after praying with Keshia, still uncertain if she was attending tomorrow's celebration. She was tempted to call Jonah but decided not to, out of respect for his wishes to not contact him. She was having such a feeling of dread, as if something was not right.

Father, have your SAY AND YOUR WAY!

As she usually did, Sharon disconnected from the internet to avoid being bombarded with notifications from the groups, that would hinder her rest. All she desired at this point was a peaceful night, hoping to escape the stress and confusion of the past week.

However, her tranquility was short lived.

Her eyes flew open!

Something was wrong!

She looked at her phone...12:05 am. Oh, it was not yet time to wake up, so she turned to her side in her attempt to go back to slumber land.

Turn on your internet connection and check your WhatsApp!

Oh, she welcomed hearing that voice, it was literally days that she did not hear HIS voice as she did what she was told. Ten missed calls from her sister-in-law, about 15 minutes ago, and a disturbing message....

"Your husband needs you!!"

WHAT HAPPENED?

Panic surged through her as she immediately dialed her sister in law's number. She picked up on the second ring screaming hysterically so much so that she barely understood what she was saying but she managed to decipher... "I don't want my brother to die!"

Sharon flew off the bed with that, demanding that she calm down and explain what happened. She sobbed uncontrollably stating, "Jonah threw Sherry out this morning and he tripped and went over to the neighbor's home and attempted to break open their house and shattered all the glass panes, and is bleeding to death, my husband is there already and they took Jonah to the hospital.... hurry and go to the house!

"Which house?"

"YOURS!" she screamed at her, "hurry!"

She hung up and immediately began getting dressed, calling Keshia at the same time as they both began praying in tongues, asking God for His intervention and mercy over this situation. Jesus help us! Have mercy on Jonah! What happened Father!!!?? "Keshia," she whispered, "I did not fight for Jonah all these years in fasting and prayer, for him to die? HE IS going to hell!"

"Sharon, we rebuke that. He shall live and not die.... that's what the Word says and that is what we say. This situation must line up with the Word of God and we cast everything else beneath our feet!"

SUNDAY 31ST JULY 2022 at 12:30 am

With Keshia on the line, Sharon raced to her former home, their voices blending in prayer as they sought God's intervention. Sharon received another call from her sister-in-law. Keshia ended their conversation, allowing Sharon to answer the call, to her wailing screams once more!!

"Listen...Jonah shall live and not die. We speak life over his dead bones now," as she began praying with her sister-in-law, she mused, who really was the pastor now, as Sharon took control in prayer for the life of Jonah to be spared. His sister was totally fearful and needed repeated reassurance of God's sovereignty.

She arrived to the entire neighborhood outside in clusters, the house wide open! Jonah's brother-in-law approached her and urged, "Listen... I ALREADY have one wailing female (his wife) in my ear. I cannot handle two, so try to be strong as what you are about to witness may devastate you."

As soon as he said it, she felt fear creeping in, but she countered it with the word of the LORD. *HE has not given me the spirit of fear but boldness and a sound mind. He will never leave me nor forsake me!*

She greeted the neighbors not really feeling the embarrassment she thought she would have felt. She looked at the damages trying hard not to conjure up the graphic images that occurred less than two hours ago. Her husband had climbed an 8-foot- tall, iron gate, with sharp spikes, pounced at their front door that were made up entirely of glass and broke it all with his left hand (he is a left hander). There was blood mixed with charred glass everywhere...on their curtains, yard, gate, doorframe, everywhere!

God, what happened?

As Jonah's brother-in-law shared with the neighbors that Jonah was unwell and was prone to schizophrenic episodes as he was housed in a mental institution for six months, many years ago! Sharon was taken aback! Throughout their years together, Jonah had never experienced a manic episode, and they had lived peacefully in that neighborhood for a decade without incident.

Overwhelmed with concern, she whimpered "Where is he?".

"He's been taken to the hospital by the police," her neighbor explained. "We had to call them due to the property damage caused by Jonah, but upon realizing his life-threatening condition, they rushed him to the hospital instead. Maybe the security cameras may provide insight into the events that transpired and answer some baffling questions." Pointing to the surveillance cameras that Jonah had apparently recently installed.

Just then, another group of officers arrived at the scene.

She and his brother-in-law, Kenny, went over to meet them.

"Who are you?" they asked her. Before she could answer, Kenny replied, "his wife."

"*His wife?* Is she the one that he threw out this morning?"

"No, that was his common law wife, this is his legal wife," Kenny explained.

"Oh," the female officer said, "Ma'am you are free to come inside once we go in and take our fingerprints and survey the area, okay?" She nodded, too numb to even think or speak. Her only concern now was that of her husband and if he made it through this; to know if Jonah was alive. She was fully aware that the amount of blood that was spilled painted a very grim picture. *But I trust you, Father, you are the Miracle working GOD!*

She ventured inside from the yard to his vehicle, to the outside walls and THEY were all smeared in blood as it told the horrific tale of Jonah stumbling back inside after sustaining detrimental injuries. She went into her home, the home that she was barred from for almost two years. It felt so strange walking back in there, after still not being in a solid place in which to live to this day.

Jesus.... why did it have to reach to this?

Entering the house, Sharon bore witness to the gruesome aftermath. The house bore the scent of fresh blood, its presence permeating the atmosphere. The tiles in the kitchen, the carpets throughout the house, and their bedroom – defiled by Jonah and Sherry's adulterous affair- were among the worst affected. The washroom was flooded with blood and water, evidence of Jonah's attempt to "drown" himself in the bathtub. The house appeared ransacked, as if a fierce battle had ensued. She sensed so much evil as she glimpsed, spiritually, a 10- foot- tall demon levitating in the living room, greedily consuming the supernatural manifestation of blood.

Firmly standing against Satan's schemes she declared boldly:

Satan, you cannot have my husband. He is destined for greatness and you cannot have his blood! Jesus sacrificed HIS blood for Jonah, and there is no more need for sacrifices, only the sacrifices of thanksgiving and praise!

The police documented the scene, instructing Kenny, Jonah's brother- in -law, to prepare the security camera footage for review. Speculation abounded among the onlookers, each with their own theories about what happened. Returning to the bedroom once more, Kenny began dismantling the camera, his visible upset revealing his thoughts on Sherry's possible involvement. As Sharon glanced at the floor, she was confronted with a sight of a seductive green negligee, tied with one of Jonah's boxers and accompanied with a side of his sock. She recoiled, dumbstruck at the lengths that Sherry would go to exert control over a man.

The once-familiar home was now unrecognizable. Jonah had spent a lot of money buying very expensive furniture and trinkets to "beautify" their love nest. Sharon's taste has always been simplistic but Sherry was seemingly high maintenance.... Sharon realized that the materialistic indulgences Jonah had pursued no longer held importance. While the house would never be the same, that was the least of her concerns. Losing Jonah that night would mean losing someone for whom she had sacrificed years of fasting and prayer. The thought of him dying in sin, while the woman responsible for their marital strife lived on, was unacceptable to her. She affirmed her belief in a God who was greater, one who had a different plan in mind!!

CHAPTER 22

WHAT REALLY HAPPENED

Sharon and Kenny stepped back outside, as the stench of blood and death saturated the once familiar house. This place, where they had experienced both turbulent and beautiful moments together, now bore the evidence of Jonah's adulterous lifestyle and disobedience to God. Sharon's inward cry and plea rose constantly: "Let him live, Father."

The two officers who were the first on the scene returned, introducing themselves as **WPC Singh 19030** and **Constable Celestine 21211.** They were visibly shaken as they recounted what they had witnessed. They had responded to a distress call from a neighbor reporting Jonah's destructive behavior, as he attempted to break into their home by shattering the door and window panes, causing fatal injuries to himself in the process. They had initially come to arrest him for malicious property damage. On venturing inside the house, they found Jonah in the bathroom, wet, bleeding, and naked, on all fours, repeatedly hitting his head against the wall incoherently and semi-conscious. WPC Singh expressed her concern, questioning if he had been shot. Admitting that she was scared, she explained that she ran out the house in fear as she sensed something sinister was in the house. She knew some form of witchcraft was responsible for what had happened to him, but quickly pulled herself together by calling the neighbors for help. She and her partner wrapped Jonah in the shower curtains and bed sheet and bundled him into the police vehicle and **SPED** to the nearest health facility, knowing every second was of the utmost importance. What was supposed to be a 20-minute drive, was done in under 5 minutes due to the intensity of the speed that she drove. They could have all been killed as they drove like it was their own life dependent on it.

WPC Singh shivered in the night air, as she replayed the harrowing episode in her mind. She asked Sharon, "Are you a praying person?"

Was Sharon ever! Lord knew all she did was pray for this man.

"Yes, I am," she acknowledged.

"Well, you need to pray as I don't think it looks so good for your husband."

Not wanting to speak the unspeakable and Sharon not even wanting to think what was being inferred!

Sharon glanced at Kenny, "Do you think Jonah will live?" after they were both privy to the loss of practically all of Jonah's life line...spilled all over.

"I hope so" was his solemn reply.

Sharon's heart sank.

I know who my God is.

She set her faith as flint.

Jonah will live and not die!

Just then, Keshia called her, the time well after 1:00 am. She expressed their fears to Keshia who shot it down immediately. They prayed together once more.

The Holy Spirit directed her to go to the main hospital in the area, as Jonah's injuries could not be handled by a small health facility.

She sped to the hospital, as she somehow knew, that Jonah would want her by his side and if he died at least she get to see him one last time. Maybe even lead him to repentance and salvation before he passed.

FATHER, be my strength!

This had to be the most difficult thing she had to endure.

She parked as close to the hospital as possible in the doctor's section. *Those security guards will not be too happy about that,* she thought sardonically.

She picked up the "anointing" oil that her sister-in-law gave her at their Good Friday Service.

NOT THAT ONE, the voice spoke to her.

THAT ONE.... referring to the healing, anointing oil from Israel, that she carried on the passenger side of the door. She obeyed.

She practically ran to the emergency entrance.

On her query, they said they did not have anyone bearing that description, but an orderly overheard the conversation and directed her to someone that came in by ambulance about a half hour ago. The health center that the two guardian angels originally carried Jonah, had transferred him to this main hospital, exactly as the Holy Spirit had directed her!

Sharon sped down the corridor. She spotted him feet first, clad in blue coverings and disposable diaper. He lay unconscious with the drips under his back and switched off. She looked at his bruised, lifeless, battered body, bandages swaddled his both hand, and legs, blood still oozing through. Trying hard to quell the feeling of fear and anxiety as she conjured up the extent of what his mortal body had to endure at the hands of only God alone knew. Sharon's main concern was for the fate of his soul, and if he had time to truly repent and accept the saving grace of the LORD JESUS CHRIST.

His body was already cold, his eyes turned up, as she opened his eyes to peer at them, his face ashen and jaws sunken as death attempted to snatch him away from the land of the living. She adjusted the IV stand and sought help from a passing male nurse to turn it back on. She then proceeded to anoint him from head to toe, pleading for the Blood of Jesus to go inside his body and begin to recharge and resurrect this lifeless, broken frame, praying healing scriptures of Psalm 41:3, Psalm 27:13, quoting John 11:4, and Exodus 15:26, whilst re affirming Psalm 103:2 to 3 and Matthew 8:16 to 17. And boldly declared Jeremiah 30:17 "I will **RESTORE** your health, and I will heal your wounds, declares the Lord..." She prayed and said, "Father let your will be done."

In her desperation, Sharon reached out to her prayer group, sharing the events that had unfolded and requested their support. Priya from India. Carmen from San Diego, and Jackie from Florida responded, joining her in prayer. She marveled at the dedication of these mighty prayer warriors, even across different time zones. What a blessing this was; whereas his sister and her husband were at home. Kenny having gone home after they parted ways, an hour before she came across to the hospital. As he said to Sharon, they needed to sleep as the thanksgiving was a just few hours away. Incredible that a celebration took precedence over a life!

She called her friend Annabelle, who kept her company, whilst she watched over Jonah, silently pleading for his life. Despite his critical condition, not one doctor or nurse attended to him as he just lay there ever so lifeless, not even stirring. She continued in prayer.

After two grueling hours, she noticed him stirring and rushed to his side. He was facing the wall on his right side, and as he turned, his face lit up on seeing her and exclaimed, "you came!"

"Yes, I DID BABY, I am here for you forever and always!"

He drifted back to sleep, as she thanked the group and updated them on his progress.

Jonah came out of his deep slumber around noon, in incredible agony from his extensive wounds. Looking at her, he gathered the strength through excruciating pain to muster up these words, "Sharon, please forgive me for all that I HAVE DONE. God said he sent me back to life so I can make corrections to Him and to you! You are my wife, and I was too foolish and dumb to see what was going on with me. I didn't understand my life or calling and did everything contrary to God and His way. I LOVE YOU. Sharon, so much!" She almost melted as she couldn't believe what he was saying, as her literal answer to prayer began to unfold before her very eyes. "I WANT YOU TO COME BACK HOME!"

Sunday 31st July 2022.

RESTORATION HAPPENED!

The revelation from the Holy Spirit she received last year about July echoed in her mind. She firmly believed that God's promises are steadfast and unfailing. With unwavering faith, she knew deep in her heart that her husband would survive and not succumb to death.

She knew then and there that her husband would LIVE AND NOT DIE...TO SEE THE GOODNESS OF THE LORD IN THE LAND OF THE LIVING!!

THE AFTERMATH

Jonah's hospitalization was extended for two weeks, but rather than receiving the appropriate medical treatment he needed, Jonah was placed in the psychiatric ward due to another misdiagnosis of mental illness. Sharon vehemently opposed this decision, recognizing that Jonah's struggles stemmed from spiritual afflictions that had plagued him throughout his life. Unfortunately, his sister and her husband lacked the spiritual insight and discernment to comprehend that the enemy sought to destroy him. Jonah's demise was always spiritual and not mental but his sister rebuked Sharon for not understanding. She angrily told Sharon that she was all new to this and that both her husband Kenny and herself knew what was best for Jonah.

Being in the psych ward proved detrimental to Jonah's well-being; as the focus shifted to his perceived mental instability while disregarding the severity of his wounds inflicted by the demonic entities that relentlessly pursued Jonah that eventful night. Consequently, Jonah's body suffered incapacitating damage, leaving him dependent on disability benefits as his physical abilities diminished, due to improper care.

After months of ongoing conflict and turmoil between Jonah and Sherry, their relationship reached a breaking point on that fateful day. It became evident that their portrayal of a harmonious union was nothing more than a façade. Despite countless sleepless nights and profound unrest, Jonah stubbornly refused to give in to the leading and promptings of the Holy Ghost. Something continued to hound them, he confessed, as he and Sherry had problems being intimate.

He began seeing Sharon's image in every YouTube video he watched as conviction upon conviction surrounded him of their wrong doings. They tried appeasing their transgression by going to "church" and partaking in communion.

GOD WILL NOT BE MOCKED THAT WAY!

They agitated each other, as Sherry threatened to leave him, which she did not as she loved the nice life afforded her. She was the antithesis of the virtuous woman described in Proverbs 31 - slothful, unholy, unfaithful and neglectful of Jonah's needs, as he would have to cook and clean and do most of the work around the home, while she slept in late and indulged in games on her phone. Meanwhile, Jonah was the best "husband" to her, buying her everything she demanded as he subserviently was to her, all he was never to Sharon.

Sherry had a health scare that caused Jonah a tidy sum of money, as she had the best treatment that a private hospital afforded.... What a stark contrast to what Sharon neglected to have, as because of Jonah's miserly attitude, Sharon was deprived of the ability to have more children.

Sherry continuously manipulated him with witchcraft spells that were placed upon him. The woman was the embodiment of pure evil, and as the truth gradually unraveled, the horror of it all was revealed. What was in the darkness was expelled as the Light of the glorious power of God illuminated every evil altar! Satan has **NO POWER!!** Only what God allows or what we give over to him.

Besides doing the dirty underwear routine, she placed stones underneath his side of the bed and under his Lazy Boy chair (a gift from Sharon for the last Christmas they spent together), and chanted that he will always be weighted down and serve her. It was revealed that their affair lasted well over 25 years. Sherry had Sharon's picture and used a mirror to "switch" them so all the love and adoration that Jonah felt for Sharon would be transferred to her as she tried in vain to

130

look like Sharon, dressing like her, emulating her and copying Sharon's latest hairstyle, at Jonah's expense of course.

In addition to these wicked acts, Sherry engaged in extra marital affairs during the times Jonah was away at work. Her immoral actions even extended to having an affair with her own niece's husband. She displayed a complete lack of shame and served as an agent of the enemy, seeking to destroy marriages. As revelations of her destructive nature emerged, it became evident that she cherished three things above all - money, other people's husbands and expensive jewelry.

The situation took a darker turn when the pastor of the church they were attending contacted them, warning that they would face a terrible accident, resulting in their deaths unless they followed God's instructions. Jonah instantly recalled Sharon's grim warning to him months before, which he had scoffed at, now realized that this was confirmation. The pastor had no prior knowledge of Sharon, and vice versa. Sherry grew fearful and feebly began rebuking it in Jesus' Name.

Really?

GOD WILL NOT BE MOCKED.

During the week in which Jonah had contacted Sharon, the Lord intensified the pressure on him to reconcile with her. He had instructed her to look beautiful because he intended to propose to her on that day. However, the conflict escalated between Jonah and Sherry the entire week, culminating in Jonah demanding her departure. He began removing all their framed pictures and made a bonfire with them.... In a fit of rage, he even attempted to heave her into the fire, exclaiming that a witch should be burned (Exodus 22:18)! The events which unfolded that week were sheer madness. On Friday night, he began praying in tongues and slapped anointing oil on Sherry's forehead that blinded her "third eye" as she fluttered around as a headless chicken, screaming in agony, "Jonah, what did you do? Why did you do that?" He was rendered speechless as it dawned upon him that he was indeed sleeping with a witch who had used magic spells to enchant and manipulate him!

At that very moment, the blinders were removed, and Jonah saw her for who and what she truly was - a devourer sent by Satan himself to destroy his life. He thanked GOD that Sharon had not given up on him or their marriage and told Sherry so. The demons within Sherry laughed and sneered as one of them entered Jonah, and despite his attempts to rebuke it, he was unsuccessful in exorcising the legions he witnessed within her, and himself!

The following morning, Jonah ordered her out the house as the demon that overtook him, transformed him into a beast. "GET OUT!" Jonah barked at her, "I NEVER WANT TO SEE YOUR UGLY FACE AROUND ME AGAIN" as he began "seeing" her for who she truly was.

After her departure all hell broke loose for Jonah, as the demon that now possessed his body began tormenting him relentlessly. He took off his cross pendant and began to bite into it like a ferocious animal destroying his crown implants, and the front of his tooth. An apparition of an elderly man, reminiscent of his grandfather, wrestled with him and then instructed Jonah to clean the mess that they made.

Jonah began spiraling out of control, with Sherry monitoring the events through the security cameras on her phone, callously observing as her demon tormented Jonah throughout the day. She made no effort to seek help from his relatives, instead desiring Jonah's death. He had foolishly included her name on his bank accounts and assets, making her a wealthy woman upon his demise – a mission she aimed to accomplish!

During this time, Jonah experienced hallucinations, seeing images of himself and Sherry pursuing him. In a state of panic, he fled from the house, stark naked **(Acts 19: 14 – 16).** He climbed over the neighbor's gate pleading for help. As he looked back, he saw an enormous portrait of he and Sherry, plastering the entire front window, surging menacingly toward him; intensifying his fear.

 "Please help me!" he cried out to the dark, silent house as he smashed pane after pane of their glass door and window; totally oblivious to the pain and profuse bleeding caused by his destructive actions. As he climbed over the gate once more, the spikes at its top hooked his left calf, ripping tendons and ligaments in the process. Jonah jumped, twisting his ankle, as he limped back home, dripping pools of blood in his trail.

Proverbs 4:19...The way of the wicked is as darkness; they know not at what they stumble...

Returning to his bathroom, Jonah turned on the shower and immersed himself under the water having an insatiable desire to **DIE!** While the water filled his nostrils, he willed death to overtake him at this point. Suddenly the water shut off! Trying in vain to put it back on, in frustration, he postured himself on all fours, repeatedly banging his head on the wall. Then, he heard voices and screams, along with the word "gunshot" before losing consciousness.

For months afterwards, Jonah remained bedridden, while Sharon tirelessly attended to his needs day and night. Just as the **LORD** had spoken to her in Houston whilst caring for Erik that Sunday afternoon; that God was preparing her to take care of her husband. And that she did, dedicating herself to nursing her husband back to health. Jonah marveled at Sharon's unwavering love and care, even after he had treated her so poorly. Her selflessness mirrored God's agape love for His children.

Day after day, month after month, Sharon nurtured Jonah, fostering his physical need with tender care.

They renewed their wedding vows "live" over Zoom with the other Standers and got re-baptized, soon after, as an everlasting covenant with GOD (THE TRINITY) AND THEM....

A TRIUNE CORD CAN NEVER EASILY BE BROKEN......Ecclesiastes 4:9-12.

Both were joyous occasions filled with love, forgiveness and the presence of the Holy Spirit.... God had truly turned all her mourning into dancing.

Today, Jonah is in physiotherapy, regaining the use of his left hand and foot, trusting God for total healing to all of his torn tendons, main veins and ligaments, and trusting for the full manifestation of his complete healing and recovery....

TO BE CONTINUED

COMING SOON...

STANDING ON S(h)IFTING SAND .... THE (GUIDE)

AND

JONAH'S JOURNEY

Made in United States
North Haven, CT
29 September 2023

42138002R00074